Minority Goth:

The Journey and Philosophy

of

One Black Man

K. L. Miller

Copyright © 2010 K.L. Miller

All rights reserved.

ISBN:
978-0615583204

INTRODUCTION

This is My Philosophy... in part. It is also one Sliver of a Truth many in the African American Community are either not aware of or refuse to believe:

Everything Evolves... even The Streets and Da Hood.

While putting this together I kept asking the Question I **know** will come:

"A BLACK MAN WROTE THIS?!?!?!?"

Yep; Deal. These are My Words... My Thoughts... My Philosophy.

And I know I am not alone. How do I come by this Knowledge? I began by Posting Online under a Pseudonym, and People Read. Eventually, I crept from this Shadow. Though to say I completely left the Dark Expanses collectively Termed **The Shadows** is an outright Lie. **I Am the Sprawl Shadows**, a naked Reality the African American Community doesn't have a clue about... and no Idea what to do with.

<u>**US**</u>. This is perhaps the most frightening aspect; Multiple Views of Traditional Methods and Ways of Thinking... <u>***all Dark and Twisted!!!***</u> Worse, I adhere to my Faith in God while bathed in said Darkness.

K.L. Miller

But that **never** Happens in the African-American Community. That's Restricted to the Streets, the Home.

The **HOME** is a Fading memory.

Respect Dominates and is **demanded**. Seldom Earned.

This saddens me and is Why I Decided to bring Honor to The Streets and Da Hood, by Crafting Tales of My Struggles to Live With Honor despite Existing within something I could not quite understand. So, I Craft Tales... and ***THINK!!!***

In this book, you'll get my THOUGHTS on these Tales... my MUSINGS. You're not gonna get organization... just Organized Chaos, and Tucked away in that stew are morsels of Truth and Wisdom.

Most dangerous of all... this Book represents an
IDEA!!!!!!!!!!!!

CONTENTS

Introduction

    Acknowledgments   i

1 Walk the Demon Path   1

2 Gen   8

3 X'an the Thought Dragon   10

4 The Wandering Monk   21

    I Think Too Much

5 The Wandering Monk   34

    What I See I Write

6 Semi-Religious   45

7 Lie of the Repentant Thug   55

8 Necropolis   70

9 Meanstreak   76

10 Seated on the Throne of Bones   109

11 The Hood Born Dom   153

ACKNOWLEDGMENTS AND THE RULE OF THREE

First... are the Thanks.

Yeah, Mom gets a nod here, God **always**. Those who helped me put this together will always be near and dear Friends...

But I wanna Rant a bit. See, if there is to be a Specific Order to the Thanks Section... Protest.

So, with the Major Thanks out of the way, let me Complete the Rule of Three:

Thank You, God for Granting me the Mind and Breath to Survive - alone, as part of a Pack, as a Human being, and for Allowing me to Suffer the Torments I have because I Know I am not alone, and someone who may Read these Words might just think otherwise.

Lofty? Arrogant?

Nah... I just wanna Thank God for the opportunity to Shake the Pillars of Human-Heaven with a bit of Street Wisdom and Twisted Humor.

He Taught me about Myself, and I will Share this Lesson. Why? Because I've Heard a guy, another Black Male, go through similar experiences. I Am Not Alone, and Our Tale is Worth Telling.

WALK THE DEMON PATH

Who is My Audience?

Everyone. My Aim is to bring Honor to The Streets and Da Hood. These are Terms. If there is Color, it is because of External Perception. The Trailer Park is Home to **MANY different Colors**.

Your Hood... Da Hood; same damn Dirt, chummers.

* * * *

Who is Minority Goth?

Start with every geeky kid in school, non-White by the Census Bureau. You know... the kid *everyone just KNOWS is gay* but has to stay in the *very **BACK** of the Closet* because within their Society (Hispanic, Asian, Black, **WHITE**), they are Outcasts, ***and this***

might just be ONE-OF-THE-REASONS/EXCUSES!!!

That Voice in your Head; the one that isn't Restricted by Being Nice... Behaving... Caring About Others Emotions.

Vicious Demon it is, especially when it's Telling the Truth.

* * * *

The Male Minority Goth wonders, "What are you Thinking when you Look at Me?"

Because there *are* so-called Normal People who Understand **some...** but not enough to Cross Over. Those are the ones M.G. can't shake Thoughts of, because if they don't Care, they are at least Intelligent enough to Remember this: keep a Wary Eye to the Darkness.

* * * *

Minority Goth... from a Black Man's perspective:

Easiest way to See as I See is Music. Certain Artists are pure M.G. Many are considered Old School Hip Hop from the First Generation of Commercially Viable MCs and DJs.

Though once the Term Minority Goth is Applied, certain Artists stand out. Like West Coast Dr. Dre from NWA fame; a Perfectionist. His Beats touch a part within Street Heads, but Listen and you can hear the Doubt within his Work; that Sliver of his Soul that isn't *quite* sure this Beat or those lyrics **truly** capture the Essence of the Moment.

And, of course, you cannot **be** Minority Goth without acknowledging the First **MC** in My Opinion to portray the inner Turmoil: Tech N9ne. It was from him that I heard Spit-Fire Lyrics with not only African-American Street Themes, but... personally, these lyrics from *Dysfunctional* say it best:

Don't you bring me nothin' Stupid

If you don't want me to Lose it

Step back if you don't want me to attack

I'm a beast; better give me Those Deuces...

<u>I've got no Tolerance for Nonsense... GET AWAY FROM ME!!!</u>

Net Sum: **YES** there's something Wrong with *him.*

That nerdy Guy with a Dream and the Drive to See it through. Something Wrong because there are too many Lonely Nights. Too many Nights and Days spent Feeling as if the Universe is sucking *everything* from the Soul, giving nothing back. And the Money and the scoffing laughter ain't shit, bro. But because of Street Training and something Inside, you won't stop Moving Forward.

But you want to... **really.** The Grind is called that for a damned good **REASON**, chummers. Worse, there are people who either turn their backs on you or Smile Politely in your Face all while your Mind Senses the Deceit and Laughter. You get so Fed Up with Normalcy and Judgment that eventually you Feel Confined, unable to breathe.

And your Thoughts race faster and faster; you See Shadows within Shadows and struggle to maintain your Grip on Sanity while trying to ignore the Laughing of your own Soul, because it sounds a touch too much like the Joker... *insane and loving every Moment of it!!!*

But because of the Confines of being Black in America... can't; whatever the Norm is... so shall you be... and by All That Is...

_NO!!!!!!!!!!!!_

* * * *

Welcome to the Clan Cursed

See With the Soul

Minority Goth - The Journey and Philosophy of One Black Man

"Writing is a Socially Acceptable form of Schizophrenia."

"Writers are not just People who sit down and Write. They hazard themselves. Every time you Compose a Book your composition of Yourself is at stake."

Both Quotes come from E.L. Doctorow, a Writer and Editor, and from my Searches, comes from the Human Timeframe 1931; like all Words of Wisdom, they are indeed Timeless, stretching as far back as the Written **and** Spoken Words. That said, everyone who ever Crafted a Word was a bit off in the head; to say they Heard Voices in their Head isn't a cruel diagnosis but a simple Function of Who and What they Were.

And of Who and What I Am; I've been Crafting Words from a very early age; this includes those Kid Poems put on hand-made Cards: Mother's Day, Christmas, etc. And yes I can honestly say I asked myself in my Head, "What should I Say?" And I can honestly say I **still** Hear Answers.

And this is a Good Thing. It means I am Thinking… perhaps the single most Dangerous Human Activity.

A Packmate once said he was amazed at how much of myself I put into My Art/My Work. I was stunned up until I read the second Quote, and now I Understand not only their Statement, but the Truth.

So, let me Introduce the Clan Cursed... the Socially Acceptable Family of Me.

Lord Silas Quick: Scion of the Clan Cursed, Professional Cook, Hurricane Katrina Survivor (at least in **this** and several other Multiverse Realities), and aspiring Writer with one Goal outside of the Kitchen: Bring Honor to The Streets and Da Hood.

Meanstreak - The Master of Chains: Denizen. Creature composed on a Singular Thought - KILLING. Known to wear two lengths of black chains from leather manacles on his wrist.

X'an the Thought Dragon: The First Great Dragon to Ascend with Thoughts so powerful that no physical Form could hope to contain them. Responsible for Teaching Mankind to Write (according to **his** Telling of the Legend), though he is still perplexed that our First Words were Pictures.

Monk: You will see many Deep Thoughts from him. Often called Wanderer or seen as an Old Man sitting by a campfire that needs no logs added to its always perfectly warm inferno. For the Price of one Tale, you Know he will share his meal and the Safety and Warmth of his fire, offering a Tale in return.

* * * *

Minority Goth - The Journey and Philosophy of One Black Man

Lastly... there's ME:

Alexander Charles Edwards... Ace to Friend and Foe alike, chummer.

I ain't pretty or Nice, just Cursed to Speak only the Truth of the Matter. So more often than not, I shut the frag up since I don't **know** the Matter, those involved, and really don't give a flyin' Devil Rat's Ass. My Job is to keep the Form I call 'The Kid' safe from himself. He's got a drekload of Power tucked in that awkward looking Human Form. So much so, that he really doesn't have **room** for anything remotely Human. **This** is where the Clan comes in, myself especially. Want the Human View? That's where you'll get it... **minus** Bullshit and Sugar-Coating.

And because of this... Silas, the Clan Cursed...

MINORITY GOTH...

HAS ACCOUNCED ITSELF AS AN IMMORTAL FOE TO FEAR AND DARKNESS EVERYWHERE... the Curse of every Idea ever Formed.

Shadows Guard you, chummers.

Here we come.

(Sanity *not* Guaranteed {{*Ace*}})

GEN

*"The word **gen** means 'illusion' or 'apparition.' In India a man who uses conjury is called **genjutsushi** ['a master of illusion technique']. Everything in this world is but a marionette show. Thus we use the word **gen**."* {{Hagakure by Yamamoto Tsunetomo: Translated by William Scott Wilson}}

They say Clothes Make the Man.

* * * *

Unless the Weather is Hot and Humid, Silas Quick, Meanstreak to his Co-workers (though never spoken to his face), tends to favor Levi Denim jeans, black Lugz Street Gear Boots, a *slightly* oversized white tee shirt and the ever-present rosary. Catch him within the confines of his Doss and the only remainder is the rosary. The Gear shifts to gray or black jogging pants and a tee shirt, with white existing as background color. For shoes, you'll catch him in socks mostly, with flip-flips serving as Doss Gear.

As for his Ride, he has none. Thanks to the Deal being Done, the all-black Honda Accord known as Wraith One has been Retired, unlike the Marker of the Clan Cursed sacrificed in Katrina's Fury: a well-worn black Duster.

Minority Goth - The Journey and Philosophy of One Black Man

Silas walks as if its weight still hung over his shoulders, though his Gaze betrays its absence with a Hole strangely black within the dark Chaos of his eyes. Yet the unadorned Levi's denim jacket does not appear out of place on his frame. The Normal dress item shimmers, and the Illusion of Normalcy is deepened within Outside eyes while inside, the Hole pulsates - a dead thing struggling for Memory-Life, pining for another Breath.

There is one last piece of Gear worth mentioning: the Hooded Sweatshirt. The *over-sized* Hood is preferred, and here is his admitted Why Behind:

> "People wanna be afraid of me. So, I hide my Face and eyes, cloaking already Dark, rapid Thoughts in something they are used to Fearing: Thug Wear on a Black Man. They may then Be Afraid... and Life can move the fuck on."

X'AN THE THOUGHT DRAGON

No problem can withstand the assault of sustained thinking. ~Voltaire

**Never be afraid to sit awhile and think.
~Lorraine Hansberry, *A Raisin in the Sun***

Here you will find... Strange Thoughts indeed.

* * * *

* * * *

Mind Droppings

Right now I could use a stroll down Decatur Street; poke my nose into the door of the House of Blues, hit Club Decatur for a brew and Chill Time with other Service Industry Types, *spin around and hit Cocaine Corner* before returning to Decatur... the part that most Tourists avoid come Nightfall. From Vampires and Lycans to Wicca and Mages of all Traditions, Normal Society Terms the Crowd there *Alternative*. This covers the Sexual Side of things nicely... for them.

Minority Goth - The Journey and Philosophy

of One Black Man

I always looked out of place, but **only** because of my Gender/Skin Color Combo; black males there were Doin' Biz or Movin' Thru, chummers. Even with My Angel and the Dancing Pixie accompanying me, I could count on someone giving me Street Looks, if not Street Respect; but that was fine by me, since I **earned** every iota of Street Cred in my Vault, ya heard? Sure you'd smell marijuana around me, but *finding* it became difficult and **not** because of Thug Street Gear: **I Dressed and Moved as all Goths do.**

Instead of the Bubble Goose... there was a Duster. Goths carried blades, **especially the Females!!!** Short Blades are wicked and messy. Close-In Fighting in the Sprawl is often done quickly and quietly... explosive Moments where the Shadows are notorious for swallowing Truth and Lies, spewing out only dead bodies and quiet Reminders that the Boys in Blue sometimes Serve as Clean-Up Crew.

See, Honor and Justice held sway over Law and Order within certain corners of the French Quarter. Ones Word **meant** something, and Money is considered the Prime necessary Evil... a Societal Plague of Man's Creation.

Enter Necropolis... and all I get are Lies and other less-than-worthy-of-Words. It wasn't Home when I was spit out into the Big Bad World and won't be, not so long as I am constantly judged and found Lacking; back **HOME** is the Big Easy.

Your Happy Ass is still breathing and ain't lookin' over your shoulder **this time...** you're Doin' Good; **that alone** earns you *some* small measure of Respect. Won't get you shit in Necropolis... except Preached down to.

* * * *

*Lord, please Pray for the Soul of this Bitch; and **GUIDE** my Pimp Hand and make it **STRONG**, Lord... so that she might learn a Ho's Place. Amen.* {{The Boondocks: A Pimp Named Slickback saying **A Pimp's Prayer**}}

Nice Scene for a Pimp... and here's what many miss in the fixating only on his Speech: Within the Freeman Home: ***she was and will be Considered a WOMAN so long as Grandpa is Lord and Master.***

The Ho? **She was actually shocked that there was a MAN within the Old Coot's Twisted whatevers**; this is the Hidden Lesson: there **is** a Difference between a Ho and a Woman.

Here is another Hidden Lesson: **Grandpa Respects The Game**; inside his Home... Woman; *outside...* you're a Ho and you Played him; **MEN** pick themselves up and do not place Blame anywhere. Survived another one, yo; Keep Movin'.

* * * *

Trust. Hard to come by, considering I've been paranoid since I can remember.

Paranoid. Why? Because I think too much. Some say I See things where there is nothing. **I Say this...**

I See Connections and have a Feel for which are Solid, not so solid... imaginary and all-too-real, yet nowhere **near** believable. **Paranoia** comes from the Fact that I'm Hard-Wired to Select a certain path and go.

Right... Wrong... none of that matters: Self-preservation of this Unit.

Trust. The Streets teach Males to *never* trust anything with tits and a twat, chummer. And when damn near every Female a cobber's encountered in a particular place has *several* Ulterior Motives behind every smile, glance and Thought, it is easy to Understand Why the Paranoia takes damn near complete control at times. Even easier to Understand Why Relationships are damned difficult, and **that** is being BEYOND Polite and Nice. Biz... there are *limits* to Trust. In a Relationship, those

Limits are, to be ruthless, one gigantic Gray Area filled with more traps than the Joker's Lair.

* * * *

I can Read a person's Soul.

I Remember Bright Souls; they are Rare indeed.

She wore Shy. For some Reason/Excuse I was angry, and this always sharpens my Gift. So when we made eye contact for the first time, this Angel on Earth, I snarled at the Lie she Wore. It wasn't in her Soul, not completely. Sliver at best.

Darkfyre Burns within her...

This means there is a **WOMAN** before your sight/Sight. Respect it or you *will* catch Unholy Hell at its level worst.

* * * *

I have yet to discover a method for asking a Black Female out on a Lunch Date *without* Sex coming up. It is annoying, but I've been turning over one possibility, and it comes from a Barely Legal Dazzle: **the Lifestyle!!!**

My First and biggest Hang-Up: ***How did you get into that stuff?!?!?!***

Not because I don't like going over my Past or sharing my Experience. I look into the Soul of the Asker, and in all too many cases, they've **been** Down the Rabbit Hole.

Since Sex seems to be unavoidable, how about Drench it with the Darkness Within My Soul? Easy to see Why I don't even **get ALONG with** most Black Females. Just the Thought of Restraints tends to drive them into near Panic frenzy.

EXCEPT FOR a few of the Younger generation (as referenced by **my** Ancient Ass); they are faced with this:

Black Male wants Gothic White Female submissive for Lifestyle; **BLACK FEMALE** looking for submissive male of any race. I remember looking at such ads in the back of skeevy, underground Sex Mags. Now? Check the right corners of certain Social Sites and a few well known and **solid** corners of the 'Trix, and just as it was in My Day, ***start looking at Teenagers!!!***

Only now, ya might wanna begin at True Teenage: ***13!!!!!***

Yah... some Topic to discuss over Soup and a Sammich, neh?

* * * *

Hugs. Simple Show of Trust.

And when it comes from the rear, at least for me, it had **BETTER** come from someone I Trust with My Life.

In General, the Paranoid have issues with someone coming up from the Rear **where we cannot See, only Sense**. In order to Protect ourselves constantly, our Senses must be always Active. This gives a paranoid the classic Eyes-Wide Nervous Twitch Look/Image - always having the Head on a Swivel.

* * * *

I will never have a Normal Female as a Lover. **DEFINITELY** NOT my Ol' Lady. Normal Females frighten me, if only because of their bland, rather shallow Souls. That, and they tend to treat Males as Paychecks and Living Vibrators. Makes those chicas who prefer horses and motorcycles a drekload easier to Understand, especially the ones who have little Use for T-Monkeys or, as Normals term them, *real men.*

Normal Females follow Porn Sex Rules: One-One-and-Done. Emotions are to be *argued* about, never really Dealt with and **Certainly NEVER** Understood. Males cannot make this effort, can never achieve this Goal and should only offer token attempts (the whole Flowers and Fancy Dinner thing, cobbers). Normal Females are *terrified of a Male who spends **any** Time Thinking*, though they **claim** to want and need their Chosen to constantly think on them.

And as proof of this think-on-them, ***BUY THEM USELESS SHIT THEY CANNOT TAKE WITH THEM WHEN THEY DIE!!!*** Shower them with Things, for **this** shows-and-proves Love.

I have yet to meet a Normal Female who did **not** look at me as a Paycheck **FIRST!!!** Humanity? Not even in the Top Ten, chummers. Considering Necropolis Locals tend to **PRIDE** themselves on being Country Normal, a **STANDARD,** is there any wonder I do not See Normal Females look upon me with anything **other than this**?

And Fear? I do not favor the stupid Mindset. I don't smile and drool over cleavage shots, and when Sex *does* come up,

Normal Females Fixate on the Restraints and leather, the Whips and other Images...
TRAPPINGS... DAZZLE FOR THE SIMPLE-MINDED.

Why?

Because I Understand Passion. Because I Understand Passion goes beyond my dick in your twat, ditbrain. I understand Dark Desires and Twisted Needs... thrice-fragged Connections that torment Souls where they cannot run, where no Materialistic Balm can *hope* to reach and salve.

And here, the only possible Dose of What-me-Worry, comes from a Human Hand... Human Heart... Human Thoughts; sometimes Dark... sometimes coated with the worst Emotional offal.

Yeah, I have a thing for **WOMEN**. Human Females complete with that Chaos Stew we call Emotions. And just because I sport A-Dick-and-Two-Balls does **not** mean my Emotional development stopped at Pussy, Money, Cars and Sports. ***I REQUIRE MORE*** from this Thing Called Life.

Put in Street Terms: Normal Females Love Hustlers, ***and a Hustler in the Game ONLY Loves dat Money, yo***.

* * * *

I ain't Normal. Anyone who has ever known me will (depending on a few Things) tell you this.

That said, what kind of Female considers me a Friend?

Strange Question? Hardly. More than one Female has a **Platonic Friend**, and this Guy doesn't have to be the Dick-in-the-Glass Case (can't **STAND** that Role and *yes* I Speak from Experience... **always**). So, Sex never comes up, right?

Minority Goth - The Journey and Philosophy

of One Black Man

Answer: The Kind of Female who considers whether or not even a *drunken rut* will fuck up something Good in her Life means she Thinks, considers others as well as herself, and is not afraid to Face the Possibility of Shit Happening. There are few Nasty Surprises. Just Shit, but that is the nature of Life, thus... Doable.

* * * *

{{Sometimes an Explanation is Required... though there is always the Truth of Knowledge: Sometimes... the Why Behind is more important than even the Asking or Answer itself...}}

The Why Behind the White Room

A Literary Explanation

Back during Katrina, the bathrooms were little more than Death Traps; only the truly desperate, vile Forms of Predators and those already consigned to Death's Embrace dared venture within. So, every time I had to Go Potty, I surrendered my Life and prepared myself to Kill Another Human Being just to Keep Breathing and *take* another Piss come tomorrow.

Before that I dossed Squatter, stealing my utilities while duckin' a Bounty Hunter sent by a Fat Italian; sounds like Movie-Qual bullshit... and is just One Tale of Many within the Big Sleazy, chummers.

Net Sum and Lesson: Stripped of Creature Comforts, Mankind tends to become a truly horrific Demon, with dark, twisted Knowledge. Such as how to use trashbags for toilets and methods of Killing a bigger, stronger would-be-maybe Foe. Yet here is also where **Humanity** can be found... in the basic Social Nature tucked away with the Fifty-Two Pick-Up we know as DNA.

Left to that, Who Knows; all I Know is that Mankind now possesses this thing called intelligence, and **that** fucks with the Survival Equation like all get out; when We as a Species were Primal, we didn't give a shit about **looking good while Taking a Shit!!!** Now, there is Arrogance, Pride along with that Little Lizard. **It** still Remembers this: *Taking a Shit leaves us Vulnerable... BEWARE!!!*

Now, we are Intelligent. We Use our Instincts and set aside a Place, and it is Secure within our Domain. For here, **MAN IS KNOWN TO THINK DEEP THOUGHTS!!!!!**... gain Intelligence and turn over its Treasures where we dump **all** of our Human Waste. Oddly Fitting.

Today, thanks to the Creeping Doom of Aging Pipes, I have no water in the Family Doss. Today, on a bright, sunny Day that fills *part* of me with Youthful

Energy and the longing to Breathe the Sun, I find my Thoughts dragging back to the Superdome bathroom and doing their damn level best to avoid That Child.

* * * *

It shall be White and Pristine, despite the Filth we Leave here; we shall Maintain it with humble diligence and quiet reverence... for the White Room is the Crossroads of Humanity... **where ALL are Equal.**

Minority Goth Presents:

The Wandering Monk - I Think Too Much

Let me End and Begin with Fear:

I Craft Tales about Psions, specifically Empaths. They possess the Ability to sift through not only Thoughts and memories, but **EMOTIONS, and thereby Know the intention... Know some of the Soul... the Why Behind.**

The G-Code: ***No Snitching.***

Comes from an old Axiom: Mind Your OWN Business; the G-Code is a Response to the collective Mentality today's Society knows/Experiences/Endures, and there is no need to look no further than the Cell Phone you're looking to upgrade to Smart-Phone status because you can't keep track of your Social Network**s**... *PLURAL!!!*

This Collective Entity now Looks at this problem: Privacy. Here's where I have issues.

Post Publicly, your Life is an Open Book. **DEAL** with the Drama/Bullshit.

Do not whine about the Loss of the Shadows once you've Stepped into such harsh Light.

Minority Goth - The Journey and Philosophy of One Black Man

For this is the Fertile Ground where Fear festers, spreading faster than Viruses, approaching Gossip/Bad News-Speed in a Small Town.

The Collective wants to know... **needs** the Raw Data. Doesn't give a shit about the Life, the Soul possessing this Knowledge/Data, irrelevant Datum to be Discarded. Always.

I Craft Tales about Empaths, and We KNOW these Secrets. We Know these Tales, Truths and Lies. Nothing is Hidden from us **unless** we Blind ourselves to the Thoughts and Emotions pushed out simply because you Exist. **Because even if there is no Form to it, everyone Thinks Thoughts; thus, we always have Something to Read and Study. We are NEVER without untold Treasures and Valueless Tidbits and Trinkets**.

To the Mundane Soul, to everyone walking around, the **THOUGHT** of someone you do not know, like or give a shit about having the Power to simply pry open your Chest of Dark Secrets... not to mention the Puppet Master Abilities; we won't **even** get into Pushing which threatens to Explain all of those nagging Voices in our Heads, some of which we've decided to Medicate into metamorphosis because we **forgot something important!!!**

Mankind **IS** Evolving. The Shadows **have** Grown long and deep. No Place is Safe.

Best to Pay Close Heed and Attention to those at the Vanguard, those dirty Souls Fighting the Battles Generals and Politicians and Power Players ponder over while doing what they do: Think ***and Control.***

Shadows Guard you and Yours this Evening and the countless infinity to come, chummers.

* * * *

Goth Chics and Thugs; this ain't about the Color Thing, but about **Emotions.** Thugs Guard their Emotions like they Guard their Money and with just as much savage viciousness. Many Goth Chics find this exciting, arousing even.

Here's the Kicker; in the African American Community **in General**, a Black Male is *never* to Expose his Emotions. I don't know How or When the occult got attached to Emotions, but it is Used heavily in the Communities I've Existed in and those I've observed.

RISK MONEY before you Risk your heart; you'll Make the Money back. Maybe that's the Logic-Flow.

Scared Money don't Make no Money...

Same applies to Matters of the Heart, chummers.

* * * *

Minority Goth - The Journey and Philosophy

of One Black Man

If you are a Dom, you are Functionally Paranoid (won't go into **HOW** Functional, since it's a Personal gauge anyhow). That said, **the most terrifying Place for any Paranoid lies Within.** Occasionally, some find this Place better than Reality; a Dom, however, is faced with bouncing back and Forth between Worlds and Social *Norms*. So it makes sense that Doms tend to have a near-psychic Knowledge of their Surroundings.

Street? You better **not** be **CAUGHT SLIPPIN'**... **Caught Sleepin'**; that will get you shot every damn Time. Paranoia is the **NORM** for every Hustler Posted on the Block/Corner. You Trust **none**, and know *just how far* you can Trust those people ya gotta Do Biz wit'; **and if it has Tits and Ovaries... not at ALL!!!** Save that Shit for if you fuck up and Get Married and Settle Down, yo; until then, Find 'em, Fuck 'em and Forget 'em. **MONEY** above all else. As for Looking Within...

You'd better see a Hard Heart if you're Out in The Streets, and it had better Show when someone dares glance into your eyes.

Kinda Explains Why a Hustler never makes Eye Contact with a Female. In that Mindset **Females** equate to **EMOTIONS** and those things Frighten them, no matter what their Lips Speak.

If you're a **TRUE** Master, you Face Emotions with the same calm of a Warrior Facing Death.

There will be Pain. This is Unavoidable... **DEAL** or be Dealt With.

That means not just looking into some dark places, **but upon Dark, Tormented SOULS!!!**

First Stop on that way... ***YOUR OWN!***

* * * *

True Playa ain't Got Game; True Playas don't Play.

Do not Play with Emotions; they are dangerous things and **NEVER** Toys.

Besides, **HONESTY** gets better results, though I will offer one Warning. There are People who believe Playing with Emotions is **part** of the whole Dating Process; these same People treat Honesty as **BRUTAL** Honesty, and react/respond to Honesty as such. No real idea Why, except they are comfortable with Lies and half-Truths.

* * * *

Let me Tell of Ra's All-Seeing Eye:

Most people will say that they see much more than they let on. I **See** the Truth of the Soul... have since the Moment I was escorted back from the Other Side by Papa Ghede as a Child. Since that Time, if I Think, or sometimes when I **don't** Think, I can Know certain Things about a Person.

Minority Goth - The Journey and Philosophy

of One Black Man

And these Things are **always** hidden deep within them, behind the massive Walls we as Modern man find necessary for whatever Reason/Excuse is viable/will satisfy the Moment. Sometimes with a glance, but not always, I'll Know things about someone that they've done their damn level best to Hide, and for the most part are quite successful. Go about Day-to-Day and no one would ever suspect, and this is how they like it.

Which makes Dating me a royal fucking nightmare. Worse, this Ability isn't limited to physical sight... far from it. Every bit of Data generated by **EXISTENCE** is processed over and over again, Puzzle-pieces constantly shuffled and re-shuffled until they Fit, the Picture examined and re-examined, Process Repeated ad-infinitum. Paranoia? Certainly, added to the very real Fact that I not only make the connections, but have enough Intelligence and Brave Stupidity to Test the Theories - to see what Flies and what falls hard.

So when I hear a Female say she's not into Girls, I can hear the so-called Ring of Truth as well and the reverb-Lie that many Normal Females have. I've lived long enough, and Experienced enough shit that I can even tell the difference in the Lies; some are Liquor Lesbians (get 'em Drunk... Party On!!) while others are just at the stage where admitting a Drunk Moment is acceptable (and all flavors of that Lie). And when she says she's Happy, I'll Know the

Lie even before she opens her Mouth. Data already processed. I've Heard the Lie before it has a chance to alter the Body's natural function.

* * * *

This is the Society we have Created:

Work brings Work-Stress. In order to not bring that trash home, we have Outside Activities. This makes Sense until we started Working from Home. Now the Trash has to be tossed out with the pizza boxes or flushed down the toilet with the rest of the shit. **THIS INCLUDES SEXUAL TENSION**; can't go Home and boink the Ol' Lady/Man when Home **is** the cause of the **Work**-Related Stress. So... *Outside.*

Shuffle the Deck a bit, chummer, and Think this shit through. There's a logical Answer if you're willing to Live within the Lifestyle a bit: **THE PERSONAL HOME-ASSISTANT!!!!**

Of course, it takes being able to See your Significant Other as Two Separate Human Beings, and **they** have to master this Role as well. However, it can Work ***if you're willing to put forth Honest Effort, as with any solid Relationship.***

* * * *

A Lady in the Streets and a Freak in the Bed:

Problem is, here in Necropolis, and in most places considered **NORMAL**, your Wife/Ol' Lady

cannot be a Freak. Wife is Mother, and Mom cannot be a Freak. It's not in her Make-Up.

Let's back up about twenty-years though and something becomes rather clear: **today's Mother was yesterday's Mall Rat, Teenage Goober/Geek/Jock/Stat/Prep, people who Carved out their own Niches then redefined them for the next generation because we were not satisfied with the Status Quo**. Remember that last part: **Status Quo;** if Status Quo is Wife-the-Baby-Making-Unit-House-keeper is the norm... it's only *NATURAL* that Females would Break with Tradition.

By this I mean Mom **is** a Freak in the bed, and she **NEEDS** DADDY to Accept this fragment of her Whole and Treat it as his Priceless Treasure... something to be maintained with Love and Attention.

The Norm? **Daddy needs to *keep* his Freak-on OUTSIDE of the Home and that means Outside Action and Lies.** Choke it down for the rest of your life, cobber. What you *__NEVER__* DO IS DEIGN to Look for a Wife capable of satisfying your Dark Needs **at Home**. This makes her a Slut and Whore (Morally Corrupt/Politically Correct Definition, **NOT** Mine).

* * * *

* * * *

Let's get one thing straight: ***<u>SEX IS DIRTY, SWEATY AND NOWHERE NEAR THE CURRENT HUMAN STANDARD OF SANITIZED-</u>***everything!!!

That said, here is the Master's Take: *because* of our current Human Standards for **Clean** we will seek it as soon as the opportunity arrives. In this, I am no different that any other Human Being. So rest easy and enjoy the filthy, sweaty, unconventional mess. By Our Nature, **we'll Clean it Up** when we are Done.

Now this Logic Flows even Internally; for some however, **FILTH** begins Within. For them, Sex will *only* be an Unclean Act best tucked away within the dark of Night. And from **these** Souls come the Tortured ones who would **share** such filthy Thoughts and **ACTIONS** with someone - ***<u>someone they Love and who Loves them.</u>*** You get Greedy Egomaniacs and Fools thinking this Clap-Trap: **Keep your Trash Outside of the Home**. For those people, Cheating is How this is Dealt with.

Never Understood that part, though I Know Where it comes from: the Old Habit our forefathers had of visiting the Prostitute to Unwind before Being Husband/Father/Good Upstanding Citizen once the Public Eye returned to his Home and Workplace, blinded by the Five-O'Clock-Rush Home Void that today's Society spawned; guess Mankind hasn't quite Evolved enough to cope yet.

* * * *

Minority Goth - The Journey and Philosophy

of One Black Man

Daddy ain't home; good thing. Wonder what the scumball would do if he Understood that his absence, his bullshit, even a *sliver* of the steaming Fresh-from-the-Hoop Shit-Pile that he Reps so damn hard is Responsible for one of the many Psionic-Scenes drifting through my Thoughts.

So many of my Tales deal with Single Mothers and nearly all of my unpublished/unposted Illegal Tales deal with Teenagers of Single Parents because they get a unique perspective on the whole Dating thing. **STRAIGHT FROM THE BOOK OF THE AMERICAN DOUBLE STANDARD!!!** Add this to the unprecedented Access to the plethora of Human Generated Data. Solid or complete gaseous methane-from-the-shit-pile, the average Illegal can get **an** Answer to any Question they conceive, though only Adult Experience gains this bit of Wisdom: ***consider the Source***.

Another thing I Speak on using this Tool, is the happenstance when the Illegal **knows** this because some of their most accessible Sources are, to be polite, Spokespersons for some seriously shitty, **sadly standard** Stereotypes. When one learns Lies from Liars.

That said, **what does one say about the Single Mom cruising the bars while her daughter is with the Sitter or Grammaw?** Nothing, because of this Assumed Lie: ***the Kid's Alright.*** Bull. Who says her daughter isn't fantasizing about all of the Wild Sex the Media tells her that her very own MILF Mommy *should* be having. We call him Hypocrite for telling his son to **not** Run Game when he's steady doing it, to keep Food in the House, Roof over the Head. We **never** mention the Playa/Hustler as Male Ho... **ever!!** And we do not Think about the lone Male Child watching Guy after Guy cycle through the Place, each treating you differently with Invisible Nuisance being the unfortunate Norm.

We give our Offspring little credit. We **created** the Tools they have, **encourage them** to strive to be Better forgetting that it takes Knowledge, Wisdom, Experience, and Survival to earn the breath it takes to **instruct** the Future on **how** to use what we've created. ***And we're Still Learning!!!!!!!!***

Asked Why I Think on the Illegals so much, I Blame the Lifestyle and The Streets. Given two People who Truly Love and Cherish each other, they **may** Breed. This means bring up a Child **within** a Home that is based upon the Lifestyle!!! So, I **THINK** about the Single Dad who lost his Wife in a tragic car accident, himself a Dom **raising a Daughter who asks about memories of her Mother!!!**

* * * *

This is part of my Issue with the Church as an Entity within Necropolis:

Minority Goth - The Journey and Philosophy of One Black Man

I've been told often to Find a *Church Goin' Woman*.

Three Words and an Oxymoron. **WOMEN** are not part of the Church Goin' Mentality. **WOMEN** Understand that there are Human Beings sitting in the pews, and the same Miss Prim-and-Proper with the Bible-in-Hand and Holier-than-thou slight smirk on her Polite Smile as she greets you *really did lose her Husband, a Good Man, because she used the **BIBLE** to justify NOT giving him head!!!!!!!!!!!!*

See, **I** can't conceive of a Kind, Loving and Caring God who **can't** give a Loyal Follower a Wife who **enjoys** suckin' Hubby's cock until Daddy is a Happy Human Being once more. **Not** this mind-fragged Ego/Emo Slut that Society keeps **demanding** he become by Thirty-Something.

THEN we get to the illegal Tales and the Stereotypes: the Black **FEMALE/Male** who was *just at Da CLUB* a few hours before rushing to the nearest bathroom to puke and somewhat freshen-up. Gotta sing in the Choir today; can't look like they did **last** time. Yeah, these are the Females I've gotta Pick-and-Choose ***My Second*** From.

Remember, the Lifestyle is just that... **A LIFESTYLE!!!** Every single parishioner **in** whichever Church I attend, at least those who know Jack-Shit about my Life Outside of Prying Eyes, knows that the Missus (and here Stereotypes become...iffy) occasionally **will** be Tied Up and unavailable. ***<u>The Joke will be ALL TOO REAL!!!!</u>***

Keep **CHURCH, RELIGION AND POLITICS OUT OF THE BEDROOM; THEY HAVE NO PLACE OR FUNCTION THERE!!!**

Might wanna add Government there too... but that Thing has a habit for Fuckin' People Up the Ass... and **all** Human need to shit... so They **KNOW** they have plenty of Possible Partners... *willing and not.*

The Wandering Monk:

What I See I Write

*This is a T-Monkey Definition for **Slut**: a Female who sleeps around.*

It is interesting to Notice what is not mentioned in this Definition: the Female's chosen Likes and Dislikes... Turn-Ons and Turn-Offs; my Definition is not so sloppy.

A Slut is a Woman who enjoys Sex. She has well-defined Limts, but within those Limits... there are no Inhibitions.

*There is also one other thing that truly Defines a Slut within my View: the Trust within herself and me... to **PUSH** the Limits... but to cross them **only** when **she** feels she is ready... success or failure... outcome be damned. This Trust extends to a failed Experiment... in that she Trust me to be at her Side as Counsel... **not** Judge.*

* * * *

Touch is not an easy sense to Define. It is, however, highly communicative. That said... it helps to Understand the Motive behind the Touch.

Too many Words can cloud the Truth; a gentle touch can hide evil intentions.

* * * *

I often watch vampire movies; there are Moments in different Films... where the Victim trembles with Fear as they accept the unholy Gift... or are just too exhausted from the Games/Torment to fight any longer...

This is something every Dom should acquaint themselves with... the Moment of Surrender.

* * * *

Nature has a Way of turning Habit into Instinct.

Perhaps it is not a stretch to consider Honor a habit... and let Nature take its due Course.

However... we are Mankind; we tend to taint/twist/alter all We Touch.

* * * *

I was Schooled to the Streets. I was Schooled to the Game. Both of these were by Male Figures... not Men.

I discovered the Lifestyle... by Accidental Nature. By this I mean: being a Dom was always within my Nature; Fate/Experience/Fortune allowed it to Grow within me.

Time and Experience has taught me this: The Streets... Da Hood... and the Lifestyle... share **certain** Philosophies.

Minority Goth - The Journey and Philosophy

of One Black Man

*Man... is a strange... and Powerful... Creation. Respect it... or you **will** suffer the Consequences.*

Life gets Lived around the Cooking Fire/within the Kitchen. Food and Drink are Life.

Respect and Honor are Different.

Respect and Power are always Connected.

Sheep Fear Honest, Honorable Men.

* * * *

Some say this is Racist; they are correct. It also happens to be Truth.

In every Kitchen there is one older Black Woman who knows **everything**. This Woman has Power; Respect it.

* * * *

I watched a Black Female listen to my Words... spoken with the Master's Tone... and the Deep, Dark Thoughts of the Wandering Monk.

It was as if she was getting a breath of fresh air... and was not familiar with its Flavor.

* * * *

Playas move as if they own the place.

Doms move with this one Thought: They are Here/Now.

Playas are Nervous; Doms are Controlled.

Lies are Blood for Playas; Lies are Last-Ditch Tools... used... but never looked upon with anything but utter disdain.

Truth for Playas is sunlight to a thirsty Vampire.

It is Breath and Heartbeat... Soul and Thought... for a True Dom.

* * * *

Despite the differences between my memories and those owned by others who may have been in within whichever memory is Questioned... there is one Thing I cannot deny: Fear has always been an important part of Growing Up.

Somehow I learned about Fear... and always asked, "Why?"

Somewhen... I decided that Fear, while an important safety mechanism... was not within me.

I believe it was when my great-grandfather told me something like this:

Fear God, not Man.

My problem with this... is that I do not Fear God; how can you Fear a Being that grants you Free Will?

Minority Goth - The Journey and Philosophy

of One Black Man

* * * *

This is the Mark of a Female who is frightened by her S.O.: she will look up and make eye contact just long enough to get caught... then, with a slightly frightened appearance, duck her head **away**.

Replace **away** with **down** and she is a Hoe.

If there is no fear... then the head movement will be down and away; this is the truest mark of a Silly Ho... one who will bring Drama.

* * * *

I was secretly watching an adult comic... back when Cable Television placed them on during the darkest hours; it was there that I head this Joke:

It must be hard to be an Atheist during sex.

Being a kid... I always wondered what people said when they had no knowledge of Christianity... and wondered if it made sex any different.

My conclusion: people were still having babies... must not matter.

* * * *

No matter how I look at it... once you introduce God or Religion in general into Sex... the Flavor shifts to Bland.

* * * *

I work with males who have a tendency of letting the Females in their lives into their Wallets.

In The Streets... this is called having someone else Count Your Money; it **ALWAYS** leads to internal stress and makes a Male two things: pissy and miserable.

Which they are; yet the solution: simply taking control over their finances... is beyond them. While I Understand that sometimes this is the case...

How about finding a Female who won't treat you like shit?!?!?!?

And each Time... the 'Answer'... is this: Appearances; gotta **look** like A-B-C.

I don't get it.

* * * *

There are certain Faces that attract Females.

Recently, the Master's Face... regardless of Emotional State... has brought interested gazes from Females.

It is Important to Understand: the looks come from Females... **NOT WOMEN**.

Taken at this Level it is easy to Understand this: not all Females are Women.

Minority Goth - The Journey and Philosophy
of One Black Man

* * * *

I was raised in the Streets; this has several advantages and disadvantages. One of the worst Disadvantages comes from a Street Axiom:

You can't take the Street from the Kid.

As I grew older and became a Man the Laws and Rules and Dictates of the Street are more important than ever... if only because I See so many throw their lives away chasing money.

It is my belief that Honor can save those trapped within the Streets.

* * * *

Say what you Mean; Mean what you Say.

Never give your Word carelessly, but **always** Honor it once Given.

These are two of the Forms I follow... and they cause the strangest reactions in people.

* * * *

I don't Flirt.

I do, however, Speak the Edited Truth. Done with the proper Tone... it counts.

Strangely... the proper Tone is, apparently, The Master's Tone.

* * * *

I recently had the Opportunity to Pull a Female's Hair.

On the down side... there was no Feeling of Ownership in the action... or her reaction.

On the somewhat positive side... her reaction: **INSTANT Compliance**; she stopped her conversation and followed.

Another curiosity: the obvious enjoyment from the act... and its inflation when she saw who held her hair.

She remarked that everyone else said hello or some other Greeting... ***where I simply pulled her hair***.

My Remark... amused me:

"Hey... I've gotta be Me!"

And in this there is Deep Wisdom... for the Master held sway the entire Shift; during this Event... each brief Glimpse into my darkness... brought interest... and that Look:

As if she were Seeing something Dangerous... and it thrilled her.

In **this**... there is cause for Concern.

* * * *

I love her... so I can say that she Spoke Honestly:

"You won't ever let anyone Love you; you're too guarded."

I am still guarded... though the guards are seasoned veterans of many Challenges... so they Know their Roles.

And one Role... is to filter out **who** gets Close.

* * * *

I know a Young Woman.

Were I to Craft in Words what I See... it would be this:

She is a Slut... but not a True Slut. She is accustomed to the Trappings and Playa Lies... yet does not shy away from Brutal Honesty... even though it scars her easily.

Were I to sum her up... one Word spring forth every Time:

Potential.

* * * *

I am considered Heartless because I am brutally Honest.

* * * *

In my youth I often wondered why Females were scared of me.

Now I Understand Why... but it doesn't change one Fact:

I am a Dom... always was... always will be.

Back then... the Master Slept.

Then... he Woke.

* * * *

These Lyrics from **Tech N9Ne** are True:

How ya gonna Fuck me on Sunday

And say you Love me on Monday?

YOU BUGGIN!!!

Sex does **NOT** equal Love.

* * * *

Definitions:

Pantyhose are Worn by Normal Females.

Thigh-high styles without garters are worn by Horny Females.

Thigh-high with garters are worn by Women and Women-wannabes.

It is easiest to Violate a Normal Female... and one need only enforce one simple Rule: unless she is defecating or is Required... the pantyhose stay on. It should come as no surprise when her Thoughts turn Dark... and Normalcy suddenly becomes on big Gray Area.

* * * *

I have watched a Woman struggle to remain Here/Now, when every fiber of her Body, and perhaps more of her Soul than she cares admit to, **HUNGERED** for her little Corner of sub-Space.

It is interesting and profound to Note that the Time spent studying the Masks we all wear proved invaluable.

THE SEMI-RELIGIOUS AND SCIENTIFIC

Live long enough...; quite possibly, the Wisest Words ever Spoken to me.

As a child I nearly died: Spinal Meningitis; I've known Mothers... Families... who have suffered though this Quiet Nightmare... and do not make light of it or the disease, merely relate what I Remember... still Burned into Memory and Soul: *from the Light came a man I thought was my Grandfather, because he Looked like him and I felt happy like when he was nearby or in my Youthful Thoughts...*

Only now do I comprehend: Grand Dad was still Alive-and-Kickin'; the Dark Figure, and he would walk at my side for many years, always seen wearing a fedora (how does a child **know** a Fedora having never heard the word attached to the Item...) and a long black cloak was, I Know, Papa Ghede.

And one of Papa's Powers... is the Ability to Read and **KNOW** a person's *SOUL!!!* As I Child, I was AWARE that I could do this... and wondered How... and **WHY**; heavy Thoughts for someone still trying to figure out Why this Girl was Cute and that one Wasn't.

And one of his Duties... is to Stand Guard between the Realms of the Living and the Spirit Worlds; perhaps this is the Excuse I should use when telling of how I came to Thoughts of me being the **Guardian of the Grey Between.** *** Definitely sounds cooler than I was a Role-Playing geek with an idea based on how I Felt about myself at the time... right?***

* * * *

God the Alien and Space-Time:

Let us make the assumption that God is the Supreme Alien.

If you follow certain Traditions, including *all* sects/versions of Christianity, then two things become frighteningly possible: One is the existence of Satan or some other manifestation of Evil. The other is perhaps even more terrifying: Spirits are REAL. That is to say, there are *lesser aliens* beholden to God and these Spirits can be access by Lower Creatures (prayers, incantation, summoning and such).

* * * *

The History Channel had a show that detailed the current Big Bang Theory, terming it Expansion.

Near the end of the program they give a detailed visual depiction of this process; as I watched I became Aware of something... maybe. **LIGHT** came *after* the initial Expansion; since the Einstein Universe has a Speed Limit of the Speed of Light, **this** is where **our current Universe**, the one bound by the Speed of Light, exists. Follow this Logic Flow and it becomes apparent that outside of the first Light Photon is *another* part of this universe, one not bound by the Light Speed limit.

This also sparked another Thought; if the Universe is expanding one of two things must be true, there is something adding to our current Universe, or the very fabric is unraveling at a pace that allows what we perceive as the Known Universe. Given the Theory of Space-Time, one coherent Fabric, either Space or Time or Both are being created or are unraveling.

Probably the most disturbing Thought is this: is there a final Light Photon behind us? That is... is our Known Universe finite as we go back towards the Center of Expansion, the Center of Everything Known and Unknown?

* * * *

Time. It Exists; it can be measured, and so, **must** be Real.

You cannot move through Space without moving through Time in one manner or another; this

Mankind has proven if only through travels into near-outer space. What has not been proven is the counter-positive: one cannot move through **TIME** without moving through Space. Indeed, Science Fiction has played fast and loose with this one peculiar Loop-Hole in the Space-Time Theory; it is my Belief that one cannot move through one and only one aspect of the Space-Time Continuum... at least with modern Technology.

Which brings up a fascinating Personal Theory: **some forms of ENERGY are capable of moving through one and only one.** As not-proof I offer not only Spirits, but the Belief in reincarnation

* * * *

Souls, Space and Time:

The theory is called Inflation; it is the current manifestation of Where-Did-it-All-Begin.

If it is true that *everything* began from a Cosmic Egg, infinitely dense and infinitely hot, then this Statement is a frightening Concept: **every soul that exists, Human, animal and alien alike, existed within that hot, dense Origin.**

According to inflation, our Universe began *first* with one rapid expansion.

If the Soul Theorem is true, then somewhere within that first expansion are Souls, since the Soul can be classified as an amalgam of unknown and known energy patterns and wavelengths at *least* on some level.

* * * *

There is no such thing as empty Space; devoid of any matter and radiation, such a region **does** contain Space *and* Time.

According to Inflation, the Universe is expanding; to my admittedly limited Knowledge this means one of two Truths: *something* is being added to the Universe, or it is uncoiling like an infinite spool of thread. Of course, I can also see another Possibility, one stemming from the Spool of Thread Theory: the Cosmic Egg hasn't **finished** Expanding. (I find this particularly interesting, and cannot help but consider it if only because of the existence of Light, which, according to Inflation, *began* at Time-Index-L) In this case, the Spool of Thread is not only multi-colored, but consist of different material, each bound in some fashion.

Now... consider Souls as part of this pattern; this brings about a strange notion: Souls existed **before** there was Life, or even the possibility of Life. A counter to this states that Souls *start* from Life of X-Intelligence, since the Soul of an amoeba or the HIV strains is, well... hard to conceive of is an understatement, at least for me.

So... let us further define the Soul Theorem by saying that Souls Existed as random energy patterns until some unknown Time-Index within the set defined by the Timing of Universe (between Time-Equals-Zero and some *highly* theoretical Time-Index which allows the complex and intricate pattern called a Soul *can* be said to be coherent.)

* * * *

Alien Faiths:

Mankind is not Alone in the Universe; Math and Science both agree on this. Now... what does Faith have to say?

Try this Theory: a sufficiently advanced Species will not have a Faith-System based on gods or a God.

Of course... this is proposed by a Species which cannot agree on God or Faith, one that seems to be evolving into scientific-based paranoia.

Try this Theory: Nothing prevents said Advanced Species from being Polytheistic, Atheistic or having never considered the Question at all.

* * * *

Religion in the Shadows

My great-grandfather died a Mason; I knew more than a few of them during my childhood, and they *all* had two distinctive Traits: they held Secrets and **Dominated** their Homes, damn the Smoke-and-Mirrors demanded by Necropolis/Church-Goin' Black Folk Standards. So consider the Source when I Recount this:

I was looking at the Bible when something dawned on my youthful mind: King... James... **VERSION!!!** Wait... so there were other *versions* of God's definitive Word...? Huh?!?!? So I asked my great-grandfather; he chewed me out rather loudly (get ready for hindsight fraggin' with Childhood Memory) but seemed to look at me as if he were only *slightly* amazed that a **child** managed to come to this Thought. This duplicity confused me until I remembered that the Masons were **ONE** of **MANY** semi-religious Orders, with the *semi* coming from the stuff I heard whispered by gossipy Blacks: the Masons knew Black Magic!!!

As I grew into my Invisible Years (Teenage Black Geek in the 1980s) I got more Information on the Masons... and came to this Conclusion: the Masons are an order of Males, and every other Construct based around a gathering of Males includes booze and loose females. So... there were at least Two Faces each Mason wore: the Socially Acceptable Pillar-of-the-Community, and the Socially Accepted Old Fart who was a bit of a scamp, a Bad Boy, or some other rambunctious Definition, back in *his* Day (which is a Polite way of saying a Dog is a Dog and will die a Dog).

Perhaps the Greatest Lesson Learned from the Masons has been this: there is a **HEAVY** Price for Knowledge and Wisdom, and this is due **BEFORE** discovering if the Source of said Knowledge and Wisdom is Holy... or so foul the mind simply **PRODUCES** God's Presence in hopes of keeping whatever remains of the Body (including the Soul) safe.

* * * *

In Voudoun, Mambo wield Authority and Power; they are also more Famous. **Infamy** rest squarely with dark mambo and Bokor, Voudoun Sorcerers; when I discovered this, something jumped out at me... during Chemistry Class actually: Bokor were **WELL KNOWN** for their Potions, and that Skill could *easily* come in the guise of being a good chemist.

I will be an Executive Chef; all Cooks know a great deal of Chemistry... and Biology, Psychology, Sociology, Religious Philosophy... and a barking shitload of other Skills. All of which are vital to Bokor in one manner or another. Then again... **every** Profession requires such a mish-mosh of Skills, especially in Corporate America.

I would often *think* to ask my great-grandfather if Masons knew any Voudou, or where to find a Bokor; remember... I am African American, so if I *really* wanted **that** Answer, just take an Ass-Whuppin' by askin' a few Old Black Women (they'll tell your Grandmother and she'll tear you a new asshole *every time*... before quietly doing this **every time...**)

This is how I came to hear of which old Black Woman knew *something* that wasn't considered Godly, but among the gossipy Black Females was absolute God-Given Bible (or Chip-truth in Sprawl Speak, Pure 100 in Ebonics-of-the-Rap-Moment); some Black Females had a spiteful streak in them, and if they had access to Black Magic... they'd sling that just as fast as a fist, a frying pan or lead. And true to the In-House/Clannish nature of most **SOUTHERN** Families... I learned which of my Female Ancestors held this ability, their Names, and Who was named *after* said Ancestors (Names have **POWER**, chummers, damn the Race).

* * * *

Even as a Child I was always Thinking... asking Questions, especially **The Most Dangerous Question in the Universe :** Why?

Not sure when, but sometime during Childhood I became Aware of this: What is **SAID** can and often does, differ from what is **DONE; toss in BELIEF** and the matter gets ten times more cloudy. And yet, we, Mankind, scream bloody fuckin' **MURDER** if we cannot get **ONE** answer-set-in-stone. This level of duplicity... stupidity... ; I am sure there are Big Words for this, but it never made Sense, so I quietly ignore it for the Moment... because I've Lived with the American Double Standard too damn long to not Recognize it snarling my Thoughts.

*Like... how come they let the old lady **KNOWN** for Black Magic onto the Deaconess board of the Church?*

* * * *

Let me explain something about **Justice** from the Afro-Samurai Series: he uses Guns First...

Anyone remember this:

... Justice Flows from the Barrel of a Gun?

Now... in the Second Movie... the Poor and Destitute... recalled Justice **fondly...**

Why?

He Tinkered... he Killed, though **only** the Number Twos; but in the End... ***everyone Knew where they Stood with Justice.***

Their God... the God of Killers.

Then... Afro came along... and He played a Different God; he let Mankind fend for itself... while he Pondered the Great Deeds and Sadness that were his Doings...

And Mankind, left to his own Devices, sets to killing...

EVERYONE.

Lie of the Repentant Thug

Lie of the Repentant Thug

By: K.L. Miller

God:

Forgive me for the shit

I must Do

In order to

See

Another Sunrise

I have Bills to Pay

I Have Things to Do

And everything requires

Money

K.L. Miller

So... it's back to

The Paper Chase

And that means

I won't be Human

I won't even be

A Bad Christian

I will be Evil

I will be Greedy

I will be Savage and

Ruthless

Looking and smelling

Like the Money I Chase.

I ask that you Forgive me

Because I don't think

There **IS** a

Way Out

If you have one for me

Minority Goth - The Journey and Philosophy of One Black Man

PLEASE!!!!

Until you Answer

Keep me Safe

On these Streets

fin

.

Let me Lie to you:

    I always wear a rosary... a black rosary; recently there are Street Souls walking around with them, swinging them as they once swung the vaunted Chain. It's fallen out of favor, mostly because of the Baptist influence bubbling throughout the Bible Belt... and because of this: everyone knows that I wear it because *all* Thugs from New Orleans wear them ... **when there is Great Sorrow on the Soul.** In the Streets, that equates to a Lost Life... and vengeance cannot be far off.

* * * *

K.L. Miller

My First Hustle: Condom Dealer.

The older kids had nosy mothers or sisters *eager* to snitch them out; since sex was a big pastime, a few of the guys wanted condoms. However, this part of Necropolis required one of two things: for you to be with an adult... or have an In; at this one Store, I made it a **HABIT** to find the comic book spire and post up, reading as many as my mind would inhale. And occasionally I buy a stack of comics and a box of condoms; yes it looked gay...

I made enough profit to leave change lying around for my mom's smokes, any candy I wanted/needed, and in short, at an age when I didn't know any better, I was Full-Blown Hustle Money. Thug By Blood, Schooled to the Game straight out the Womb.

How else was I gonna feed my comic book habit?

Looking back, looking through Moral Bull and all of that, I don't have any regrets. I even remember the Logic Flow I had back then: so long as my friends and the guys they hung with were gonna be fucking... why not help them be safe and profit at the same time? And it wasn't long before I was selling to the White Girls I hung around, as well as a few of the White Guys who wanted to remain *strictly hidden* from actually entering a pharmacy and buying them.

Never got caught because no one suspected; Word-of-Mouth would only get you so far; I'd set up a complex system of go-betweens and such, *all for condoms!!!* Of course, it also worked well for Information; this I found out because of something that, to me, was and **IS** instinct: Don't Repeat **ONE WORD** of what is told to you In Confidence.

So... when Girl X confesses of Interest in Girl A, while being in a Relationship with Girl A's Brother (who happens to owe someone I know money)...

I heard everything and Nothing; stayed in the background mostly, and I have serious doubts if anyone from that Time remembers me at all. Funny, since that was a Time when you *had* to Talk to someone...

* * * *

K.L. Miller

Why do you wear a rosary?

I lost much in Katrina... and I am Speaking about that without a dollar sign attached to it. Friends... Fam... **HOME**; those are Things that cannot be Bought and Sold without Paying with Blood, Heart and Soul. Until I can return to New Orleans and Lay my Bones to Rest, I **must** Remember...

Now? Now I look like the Thuglings... except I don't Mr. T; there is only **one** Rosary around my neck and it serves a Purpose that will **NEVER** be Bling/Flash/Fashion Trend.

Now... there are Thugs who are asking God *openly* to forgive them as they Grind On... as they Trap or Die; **they** only wear one... and unless Gang Biz calls they fly the Colors I wear daily: Black and White. And if you look closely into their eyes you'll see them desperately grabbing for Hope, because they Know that once Hope dies... there is nothing left. Nothing...

But so long as God keeps us Alive one more Second... Grind. Hustle. Keep Moving Forward and don't let Hope die... even if it means your pathetic excuse for a Life.

I wear my Rosary, begging God to let me Know I am not Alone... that I have made a Difference... done some damn good with the Time I waste in the Here/Now. I wear my rosary because if God is Love then my happy ass needs a constant Reminder that he is not Forbidden to me... that Love can be mine.

And where you see only Bad, know now and Forever... there is a Creature of God behind the baggy pants and Thug Screwface. That Hardness is one Layer above Nothing; no Hope... no Dream... not even God's Eternal Might and Love can penetrate this Place, and we are **SO DAMNED TERRIFIED THAT IT IS THE ONLY THING WE HAVE...**

Because this entire World offers little: Money, Power, Respect and Pussy; and the *only* Way to get that is Hustle. Legit or Illegal, someone's gonna Get Shook. Some Win... some Loose; that is the Nature of the Game and so long as I'm breathing, Play. And in that case... Go Hard... or Go Home.

K.L. Miller

YOU TELL ME... WHERE THE FUCK IS LOVE IN ALL OF THIS?!?!?!?!?!

I wear my Rosary... to Remember.

* * * *

I never Banged; never Cliqued-Up...

I was Raised in the projects, the Early Suburbia/Hood/Projects-to-be Housing Projects/Micro-Suburbs, and around the Drug Game. All Gang Experiences come under a frightening thing many are struggling with: Pressure from the Gangs and your ass ***is just playin' in the Front Yard!!!!!!!!!***

That said... I was Raised and Schooled by Crips; they have that Street Loyalty...

So living in a city that is Blood-Up... feels like being surrounded by enemies everywhere you are, and your ass in In-Cog-Negro.

Minority Goth - The Journey and Philosophy of One Black Man

<u>If you've NEVER Picked up a Street Flag, DON'T.</u> Taught that by more than one **BANGER**, so I take it as Chip Truth; still... one of those Crips also Taught me this: some people *just wanna be STUPID!!!!!!!!!!!!!!*

Set-Trippin' was the Old Term; don't give a shit what it is now; see... there's a New Flag... New Colors: Black, Gray and White.

Wanna know the gang Name: Minority Goth... ***<u>LEAD BY GOD.</u>***

Ain't pretty Angels walking High-and-Mighty, just average You-and-Me doing damn good to not snap and go Crazy considering the excesses, Lies and other bullshit that passes for Normalcy; and somehow we're supposed to Find happiness in this shit-pile.

But remember... In-Cog-Negro; God snatched me from the Gang Pile... kept me safe... **and my Eyes and Mind Razor Sharp and Open...**

So while part of me wants to tell the throng of Red to set down their Flags and those Lies...

Part of me... the Young Kid listening eagerly to the Crip School him on how to cock back a Nine-Mil while cruising through Compton in a Jeep... when the driver spots a small group of... "Slob-Ass Niggas..." That Part knows it is in Danger and has to make it Home...

So... it prays to God, and it filters through the Adult... the Big Sleazy hardening... the other Wanderings, Places, Faces and Memories... until the Lie of the Repentant Thug becomes the Words formed in my Heart.

"Lord... Forgive me the Heinous Horrors I visit upon your Creatures just to see another Glorious Day in your Presence. Amen."

So. **NOW** you Know Why there's a **black** Rosary over my Black Heart.

The Flag **I** Fly.

Minority Goth - The Journey and Philosophy

of One Black Man

* * * *

Break-Ups happen, but here's the Thug-Twist: **Break-Up** is *only* used when the Male fucked up and invested **TRUST** within the Relationship; there are Songs about **Hood Males** in the Aftermath of this, but the ones that stray near Thug always end with the Male in The Strip Club...

I've Haunted those Shadows and Know a few Excuses, but this is the **REASON**: Reset the Mentality.

That is... when the guy Posts-Up in his Favorite Position, he's looking for and Emo-Dump: a Female to be **used** for Sexual Exertion, and to dump the last Relationship Drama on.

* * * *

Thugs don't Pray like Normals; they Hold Conversations with God.

Not Confessionals; sometimes these prayers become Shouting/Screaming Fits... because we just don't Understand.

This bullshit Existence has us bouncin' off the fuckin' Walls and we **know** there's a Way Out... but... *where?*

At some Point we get to Feelin' like we're Drowning in the Good Life; what's left? Where is the Sweet Air?

Funny thing is... eventually a Thug will come to the Question of Females, and **here** is the Truth many Blind themselves to: Rap Terminology has become Chip-Truth for all too Many. Hoes... Bitches... Tricks... and the List and beyond; but...

WOMAN...

She is the Answer, and in **WOMAN** lies God's Answer: Love.

Woman: The Evolving Puzzle.

Takes a MAN to Figure out *this much*...

To many Thugs, only Way to be a Man is to **shed** Thug Ways...

EVOLVE... OR GET GENETICALLY DEALTH WITH.

God's Rule of Here/Now, chummer... not My Opinion.

So. There's the Answer; the trick is Seeing this Truth within Forms you've Trained yourself **not** to Trust.

* * * *

There's always an After.

And After a Thug Prays he's gotta lift his Head and Eyes and Face Forward; he's gotta get off his Knees if he knelt down...

And then, Take That Step Forward.

So then, Foot Work is important; Gear shows how much we Care about the First Lie of Foundation: Stand on your Own Two Feet.

Reality is the Ground is Shaky, and the nagging Sensation that at any given Moment you'll be On the Run; Reality... you can't remember if your eyes weren't darting around behind closed or nearly closed lids, because even in Prayer...

Someone's Watching...

After; Thug shakes it off, a chuckle before fumbling for the Blunt and a lighter; Money-Time Ticks away, the Sound comforting, annoying, and more constant than your own heartbeat it seems; so you **make it** Your Heartbeat...

Minority Goth - The Journey and Philosophy of One Black Man

Back on The Streets... Back to The Grind.

Thank you, God, and Keep me Safe.

Amen.

Necropolis - City of the Dead

Necropolis : the City of the Dead; Here/Now, the dead include Ideas and Ideals. Necropolis is where I was spit out into Real-Time; I learned about the ADS, the American Double Standard, while memorizing my ABCs and 123s within its domain. I remember parts of that Moment, and one part in particular: the Moment where I **chose** to be as Honest as possible, not a two-faced schmuck like damn near everyone *in* Necropolis; I remember this Moment because I was a Child, and it is still one of my Earliest Memories. It is also the Moment I Broke Tradition; see... because of my high Intelligence and African American Birth, coupled with my nowhere **near** mug-ugly Thug-from-Birth Natural Screwface, I was **SUPPOSED** to be the Happy House Nigga... or the Push-Over. Unfortunately, I was smart enough to recognize Fear.

Miss something? Fear; this is how a plethora of African American Females raised the pack of Males around my current Pushin' Forty. Start with Fear, impressing upon the Child that Fear equals Respect and therefore, Love. Even as a Child, I never got this; I remember *thinking* to Ask God how I was supposed to Honor my Mother and Father when they **needed** me afraid of them? What made me such a threat; I was a **KID!!!!!!!!!!!** A Kid who figured out he couldn't Love **and** Fear God, so he **chose** to Love... and that meant to Trust Blindly. Done, and I was just a Kid; best damn decision I ever made, honestly. The instant I did, **_nothing in the World of Man can inject Fear into my System. Period._** Massive Monkey-Wrench in the Engine tasked with Pumping Out Another Unit, right; worse, Black Females have no **direct** Power over such a Male.

So... they use *Influence*...

That is the politically correct way to State: *they Fuck with a Nigga until he explodes!!!* And the more the Male seeks non-violent, non-threatening Escapes the more they fuck with everything they can, searching for the Trigger. Now there **is** a **Universal Trigger**, but Going There guarantees nothing less than Chaos:

WHY CAN'T YOU BE NORMAL?

* * * *

Every time I try to Craft something Reasonable, something that sounds Intelligent and carefully Thought-out, I start Ranting; this is a Pointless Question and does not deserve punctuation or even the leftover-Thought ellipse. And yet it does serve one Purpose: forces **everyone** to Define *Normal*; I Define it as whatever the Masses Think; massive Loop-Hole there, since the Masses think more sporadically than Chaos tolerates, which is how we get sheep in the first place I suppose.

So maybe **this** Explains *Stereotypes*; that or it's an Excuse for them; either way, the only thing I **Know** with definite Experience is that in the Standard African American Community of Necropolis, **I AIN'T NORMAL... PERIOD.**

* * * *

So... if I **had** to Craft a descriptive paragraph about me and make is as accurate as possible, what would it look like?

Even at his age, Silas looks like a Nerd; this doesn't come from ungainly dress or a speech pattern packed with Techno-Babble and Private Jokes; his eyes, even with their standard marijuana-red-haze painted over the whites, seem to always be pondering something. Broad in scope and grandeur or just Trivial Data Pulses, his eyes betray a Thinking Mind even when laughter pours from his lips and lungs, a rare occurrence indeed. Then he moves, and the Nerd Image disappears; in its place is a Form that does not have one particular set of movements... unless you call the eclectic array of Hood Born, Pure Corp Business-Type, OG, and that stutter-step that reminds most of someone slightly intoxicated or, because of the very specific focus deep within his eyes during some of those same stutter-steps, a tradition known as Spontaneous Busting of Move.

The rest paints a better Picture, but the end-result will still be incomplete; this is but **one** Example of Why so many people feel uneasy around me; nothing about Who and What I Am conforms to _**anything**_ considered Normal **if you put the entire Picture together!!!** Target Fixate on one thing, and I make Perfect sense, but any Conclusions drawn will be ass-wrong, and **that** is not my Ego, but Hard Experience.

* * * *

It is much easier for Necropolis Locals to see the Outside and **ASSUME** the rest, placing it as God-Spoken Bible Truth; the Truth of Who and What I am disturbs them, because as _they_ see it, _**I am an individual with a Thinking Mind and the Will to not only Do a Thing, but the Patience to WAIT. This makes me Dangerous, and Dangerous Things must be Killed.**_ I think the more P.C. term is Deal With, but we **ARE** in the South, chummers. I honestly believe if I wore more outrageous clothing I'd be shot on site by the Local Law Enforcement; there is a **very real Sense** of Normalcy at **ALL** Costs, Souls included.

Now, this has **NOT** stopped me from dressing and appearing as I Feel Proper; this Image hasn't been Named, though I've Crafted a Phrase that fits: **Lie of the Repentant Thug.** There is one Defining item for this: a Rosary; I wear it to Remind me that Love is not Forbidden. Many are attracted to two aspects of Catholicism: Guilt and the get-out-of-Hell-with-*Payment* that is Confession (as taught to impressionable young black males by Bible Thumpin' gossip whores; the Older males just got this odd expression and said, "Catholics are... *strange*."); whatever the **Excuse**, a Black Male with a Rosary means trouble to the Cops, especially with some Gang Bangers now sporting a Rosary.

* * * *

    Necropolis is packed with Churches; this comes from a Time when **Church** was a way of Community-Segregation. See... the Rich did **not** rub elbows with the Poor if they could help it, even in God's Presence. So it comes as no shock that such foolishness infiltrates it way to the so-called Poor and **their** Churches become Sub-Divisions within the Community-Whole.

    Now, Dim the Lights, Step into the Shadows, and the Rules follow **Shadow Rules**; that is... Rep and Blood-Line betray much and is Key-to-Lock on many *occasions.*

    Like the Southern Tea Ceremony, a Southern Sunday Tradition; sure there were Kids running around, but I'm sure I'm not the **only** Kid to figure out that there were certain Places where Certain People, People with Power, did things that made Adults tremble, **and those places were *always* kept Dark and Cool.**

Minority Goth - The Journey and Philosophy of One Black Man

Those were the Places where I enjoyed Playing and I got caught often; yet I always Remember Aged, Bearded Men gazing at me sternly, and I'd meet their gaze for a While before turning away, snarked off that they dared Judge me for wanting to Know.

Thus it is that I came to Learn Stealth beneath such stern Gazes; here is where I first encountered Adult Duplicity at its Finest and *quickly* Mastered Existing In-Between... in the **GREY BETWEEN...**

Meanstreak - The Master of Chains

I am Meanstreak. Master of Chains.

You will not see me surrounded by Males and Females; you will not see me as part of any Group, and yet Norms Created me.

Recall the Soul you tormented, picked on until they fell Silent; Remember the Silent Soul, for there are Words heralding them...

"It's always the Quiet Ones..."

Remember the Soul stood up on a Date; do you remember snickering? The Jokes? The Soul does... I Do.

Minority Goth Presents

Meanstreak - All Too Human

She has never Read these Thoughts; others may read before her and to some degree, this is Appropriate.

* * * *

Minority Goth - The Journey and Philosophy

of One Black Man

I sploshed through the near-Flooded French Quarter, smiling like an idiot as other Tourist...

OTHER Tourist...; the last time I was here...; Memory flashed back to a Walk Home in the rain and a horrible Flashback of the Decision I Forced upon the Woman I Love: Stay and Die... or come with me and MAYBE **SURVIVE...**

"You've Weathered many Storms, Wanderer..."

The *Place d' Armes*... St. Louis Cathedral; I Listened to the Spirits, even those tormented and Damned... eternally Restless... and those who Know the Big Easy as Home and see no Reason to leave the City they Love.

I stepped into the downpour, black save for my semi-soaked white socks and the brown cigarillo sizzling beneath the drops that hit the cherry when I lift my desert-style black cover to allow the smoke to drift Smoke-Signal style. Jandering through the Quarter with half-a Mojo-Stick, my Soul laid bare before Marie and Those Who Do Not Sleep. They tore memories from me... forced me to Feel.

My Angel Screamed at me, for she is not Designed to Survive; she is to be Adored. **LOVED**; there was little Humanity there, just an undercurrent of Primal Savagery that I could not shake within the Superdome. Already Death moved with casual Street Cred Swagger; I don't remember looking into her Eyes because I Know what she saw: someone perfectly At-Ease with the fact that every Smile held eyes you may well have to snuff the life out of just to keep breathing. She is accustomed to Male Posturing for **SEX/PUSSY/EGO...**; every single First Encounter was Life-Death: the Hustle and Grind for Serious Pay.

When they Called for Women and Children, I actually Felt like a Knight filled with Chivalry; I was crushed when, looking back... I Noticed that she did not look back, in fact, seemed to force herself to NOT look back...

And then...

* * * *

OK... so you WANT her to have an Emo-Fit... in the middle of this Nightmare?!?!?

How about you Concentrate on the very **REAL** *Maybe-Death that is one Too-Pissed Soul Away; if that racist joke about Too Many Niggas was* **EVER** *a sickening Reality, you're ONE-of-the-MANY, chummer. Choose... are you Meat?*

I've got shit to do... and Honor to Bring to the Streets.

My Arrogant Ass... there were my First Thoughts; next... I tossed God a Prayer for her and apologized for the shit I had to do in order to see her again. Maybe.

Minority Goth - The Journey and Philosophy of One Black Man

There wasn't anything Human in me **and I was Liquid Cool with that. Later for Human Thought...** and I never once Thought of Love or Tomorrow.

I don't care that nothing happened; being there... Feeling Good... Solid...

Sober... there are No Excuses... not even under outrageous Circumstances.

Left to Survive I am not Human and that doesn't bother me... then or now; but the **FACT** that this Place... this Mentality... will not leave me...; how can even an Angel love such a Twisted Soul? Is **THIS** what it Truly Means to be Human?

Try having those Deep Thoughts running in the background while you're Making Friends for survival-purposes; I knew enough to steer clear of the twits looking for weed openly; Dealers in these conditions either Tuck or have a Crew. I used a Charm I tended to reserve for Memory: Political.

* * * *

I Think on My Angel because it has been some time since Katrina; I Thought on her as I Remembered us walking through Our Haunts... some the same, some... sadly Different, even to the Feel of its Soul. I Remember the Imagination: me wiping her tears away at the Different... at us Forging New Memories.

I Think on her, pulling her away as I gleefully crush those Lies, bitch-slapping Tomorrow back because Here/Now... I was Zero-Cool and Liquid Smooth.

Corner Learning

This is a Typical Cook's Morning... especially for anyone with a Touch of Minority Goth:

* * * *

Inhale... stretch... and Sex is On-the-Brain; before it completely fades marijuana fills the lungs, Alerts the Senses to Reality.

Back at this shit, yo...

* * * *

Used to be... a Soul rose and inhaled Fresh Air; don't know what the fuck that is; time to fill the System with Go-Go. The First Program run is *always* Re-Up the Fuel System, damn the cost to the System as a Whole; cigarettes... that First Drink of the Day... the half-blunt/roach/last hit from the Bong; otherwise...

I Ain't HUMAN!!!

Come a long way from that fresh Pot-o-Joe, and don't be surprised if the Image of Father with the Pipe and Newspaper doesn't get a Hood Make-Over:

* * * *

It is perfectly Normal to feel Bitter once Love has Stung you.

Choking it down hurts, but is, *apparently* Necessary.

Hood Rule: Rebound Pussy/Penis

Ask me, this is Why Strip Clubs and Hoes Exist; keep that shit there and you'll be Fine. Find some thing Human-Shaped and treat it as Humans treat everything: no Thought of Compassion or caring; pure Me-Moment, chummers.

Of course, this means not Playing With Emotions, and here's something everyone must Know about **Rebound Sex: *you're Fuckin' with THEIR Emotions because someone fucked with YOURS!!!***

Petty Vengeance, pure and Simple.

Just what I See...

* * * *

Tip for the Female interested in a **Pot Smoker...**

Congratulations on Noticing the Differences: Pot Smokers are Cigarette Smokers: they Smoke to satisfy that oral Fixation; they Toke Regularly, though to call them Super-Chiefs is wrong. In *Polite Circles* the Pot Smoker is gossiped about for their Habit...

WEED HEAD is the fruity-yum-yum brah ya *smell* before you **think** to see him come around the eighty-eight corners of whatever maze he just weed-swaggered through.

* * * *

Here's something everyone can relate to: seeing something considered **FOOD** and Thinking this Thought:

HIGH.

This does not mean that I think everyone Smokes Marijuana...; it touches on something Primal actually:

<u>Under what conditions would you put THAT into your mouth?!?!?!?</u>

High.

Thus...

Being High... this Mental State...

Genetic Memory-Need?

Minority Goth - The Journey and Philosophy

of One Black Man

* * * *

Racist? No; I don't like **MENTALITIES.**

Black Bitch **MENTALITY...**; like this Black Female I encountered yesterday, and so many times in my Past that I have a Programmed Response:

I understand you may well feel that the entire *fuckin'* Universe owes your stank ass for sucking up precious Life-Giving Items, but please refrain from looking at me as if you've just seen a slimy piece of regurgitated cat-shit; tends to put me in a Negative Mood.

* * * *

Street Armor:

Pants

Don't like the hang-below-the-ass favored by the Trap Star sub-culture; the *slight slack* look is and will always be, in My Opinion, Sprawl **STANDARD**; your Pants require just enough slack to allow for some other, thinner leg covering (jogging pants, thermals, etc.)

Carpenter's Pants are not Required, though this is where I'd begin armor Selection; **POCKETS Plus Functionality: Cargo Pants** suggest (to Norms, especially their Legal Devices) that Street-Warrior Mentality Law-Abiding Citizens are Taught to Fear.

The Hoodie

Mandatory; the cut is always one size too large minimum; select a size that always your clasped hands to hang naturally, a slight flair at the elbows at Sword-hilt level is best. The Hood itself is a matter of preference, with Minority Goth Style leaning towards over-sized masses which do not rest on the head, but slide occasionally, giving the Samurai's Illusion.

Kicks

The Streets are Hard on everything; this said, only boots with a *proven* Track Record of **personal** experience should be worn; for my part, this explains the solid black Lugz.

Cover

The Baseball Cap is an American Tradition, so expect it to find its way onto a True American Oddity;

I will wear one, but I prefer the Skull Cap. Style is one Choosing Point; Function is another; jungle-style mil-spec covers fall under the same category as the Farmer's baseball cap: the one he *never* washes and seems to magically have the hidden cigarette he can't remember putting there, just *knows will be there.*

Gloves

No matter the Weather, I've been taught as a Young Child: always have a pair of gloves around; back then it was because you never knew when you'd have to Work Hard with your Hands; these days **WORK** has some very Dark Meanings. This all Said, here's the Minority Goth Take on this Tradition: **You Seal a Deal** with Bare-Hands; thus you learned to Sense the World through a Filter, and if you Made Your **MONEY** that way, the Gloves **became** your Hands, thus representing this:

My Hands are Legion; I manipulate many things *and leave no Trace behind.*

Belt

Many African American males despise the Belt; blame Whippin'/Beatings for this **before** you go lookin' for any other Urban Source.

I do not like to go around without a Method of Restraining someone; belts do nicely.

Beards

I wear a Goatee and keep it Ragged-Neat; the **Ragged-Neat** Style can be traced to The Islands, and many Stereotype Marijuana users. So... if you Toke... expect Legal harassment; most Minority Goths only Social-Norm their Beards for High-Profile Events where such casual comfort is rude and offensive...

* * * *

Stereotypes. Double-Edged...

So it must be said that I will not Define a *type* of Female Who finds something appealing about a Soul within the Minority Goth subculture; I **will**, however, Comment about Black Females:

This is the Broadest Stereotype and is **purely** Racial; got even a smidge in ya... *counts.*

From here... I jump directly to an issue guaranteed to Start Shit: **Black Women. Unless**

she's 50+ with at least the possibility (within Shit happens) of Grand Kids, you cannot have a Black WOMAN...

At Best, Lady is the Term; this explains the Habit of never being without either a Blade or some *real* Street Fighting Skills tucked away, right next to this Little Girl within her Soul; mind... she'll Defend this Spark Within to the Death. So if you Seek Prey, be Warned.

Now here is something *else* about the Term Black Woman; if you Listen closely in your Thoughts, **you'll hear the Word *OLD*...**; there is **AMERICAN** Tradition behind this: the Old Black Woman; from Good Witch to Evil ol' hag whose Name you were taught, but told to never utter (bad Luck), the Tales are *legion* of being frozen in place or Cursed by... **the Old Black Woman...** ***the Woman with Dark, Terrible POWER at her disposal.***

* * * *

Let me, the **Kitchen Dom**, Address the Public:

Most of My Tales are for **COOKS**; Servers won't like the Bias, but we've been at each other's throats since the First Kitchen: ***the CAMPFIRE!!!!!*** The Public is interested in the Sex and Gossip and Behind-the-Scenes stuff for whatever Voyeuristic Reason/Excuse/Lie-backed-by-Moral-Superiority-Complex.

I *Edit* the shit outta those Works because there are Thoughts and Mentalities within the Service industry that unnerve so-called Normal Society, *which **WE** Know as The Public...*

Like this one:

The Servers get enough Ho-Treatment from Management and the Line, ***PLEASE TIP if you, THE PUBLIC, insist or just can't help/get yer Rock's Off adding to this Treatment.***

Or... Thought on a Free Meal: ***YOU AIN'T PAY FOR SHIT. WHY ARE YOU SURPRISED WHEN YOU DON'T*** get ***SHIT?!?!?!?***

Can't Speak those Thoughts, and considering how many people now posses the ability to semi-read Body/Facial language you'd better have a damn good Mask, chummers; so Lying becomes Biz-Skill and if you're Good it Pays the Bills.

Now. The Lifestyle enters into the Picture because of simple Kitchen Life... and something I've Noticed: **Life happens in the Kitchen.**

Think about the Stereotypical American Family... even the Huxtables; in the Kitchen there was something *RAW* within the Kitchen. Gather People around the Cooking Fire and those Society Walls melt away. Don't know How or When, but Servers... even WAY-WAY Back... got attached to Sex; Cooks discovered Food is Good, and one probably got jumped for a particularly good meal. Cooks Know

Minority Goth - The Journey and Philosophy

of One Black Man

Fire and Smoke and Ash and Shadow; Flavor is Complex, even in simplicity, and this also happens to be how Passion Works.

In All Things... Balance...; coming to such Knowledge, let alone the Wisdom Behind/Around/Within, ***there WILL be Sufferin..***
THERE WILL BE PAIN.

DEAL.

* * * *

Many say I am Racist; this is because I **do not favor** African American Females.

Of course those same Sources tend to believe in treating Females, **all Females**, as Cum Dumpsters/Hoes/Hood Rats/Gold Diggers and think I'm **WRONG** for wanting ***MORE*** from a Female. Love is either an Unfortunate Accident or your stupid ass was just *looking* for an Excuse to Loose Your Mind.

That's from the Males of course; **FEMALES** (African American) think I'm Racist because **I don't Respond as the Streets/School/Da Club has told them a Black *MALE* is supposed to Respond to the Image they Project.** When I don't look at the Booty Shake, *must be Gay*; when the Crab-Attitude gets their Heads Torn Off: What's **WRONG** with *HIM?!?!?*

Heard that once from a Chica back in the Big Sleazy; **she wondered how I could be Thirty-Something, Black, Single, No Kids and No Charges!!!!!!!!!!!!** She actually asked me, "**WHAT'S WRONG WITH YOU?!?!?!?!?**" At first I was slightly offended; then I asked myself about her Male Selection and got a Sobering Truth: fuck-near every Male she could expect to take-a-likin' to here **IS** a Felon... and many are damned **PROUD** of their Records; Baby Mama/Daddy Drama is the **NORM** to the Point where there are **Spoken Rules** with How-to-Deal-With-Dat-Shit.

So perhaps *that's* Why I long to Return to New Orleans; the Rules were Passed down by Experience; Loyalty actually Means something and actually comes **before** any Definition of Love. Here in Necropolis, for **SOMEFUCKED UP REASON/EXCUSE, PUSSY RULES!!!** And before **FEMALES** get pissy... Pussy Rule, *DICK* Rule: same damn Stupidity Reigns; Egos come before **MONEY**, and to a Playa, even a Wannabe, that Dog don't Hunt.

* * * *

Flirting Shadows

I'm learning to Flirt; that is, I'm learning to be more Successful with regards to **NORMAL** Flirting

Methods. It is slow going, but I have an unusually large Skill Set to borrow from... like my Shadowrunner Skills.

* * * *

Chatting People Up is difficult; if I have no Use for you or do not like you I won't ask how your Kids are doing. Besides... esoteric, odd Knowledge is more attractive to me. Yes you have a Favorite Color but is there a Tale behind it?

This is not an Issue with Pack, though it does bring up interesting Situations.

The hardest part comes in **avoiding** Sex Talk; it doesn't get any easier since I'm a Dom and Live Within the Lifestyle, though admittedly a mild (by comparison) Slant to the more commonly known-but-never-mentioned Imagery. Yet Sexual Innuendo is the Foundation of Flirting, and thus the Lifestyle inevitably comes up. Fortunately, I came across a Vanilla Kink: Lingerie.

The Media portrays such Clothing on Impossible Bodies; where once it was Photographer's Skill, now it's Photoshop the fucker and run with it; we're on a deadline!!! Funny thing is, and I Thought about this as a rising illegal just discovering Sex, **NORMAL FEMALES** were seeing this; if they didn't Look *exactly* like the Image Shit Went Bad. So I removed the Perfect Bodies and substituted Normal: teachers, people in Church when I was bored senseless (quite often... if not *always*), and nearly every Female I happened to come across just Motivatin' Along Day-to-Day.

One thing I discovered: if it didn't Feel right in my Gut, I dismissed the Fantasy. Remember this, as Age and Experience only deepened this within me, until it is now Truth. So when I say, "I wanna see you in lingerie..." one must understand: **it is the COMBINATION** that interests me. **YOU** in Lingerie.

They say Clothes Make the Person; only Women, Sluts and Whores wear Lingerie (just check the ads if you think I'm bluffing); **I** Say The *Rule* is this: The Outside must match the Soul and *this* is Why there is a Stain on Lingerie... all because of the last Female Type within the opening Statement: **WHORES.** Why not Slut?

The American Double Standard; it allows a **WOMAN** to dress in such a manner in order to Get Laid (hence we have MILFs and Cougars); that said, such Gear is meant to Arouse and Seduce, which leads to this Conclusion: **she wants Sex.** Fine... I see nothing Wrong with Advertising, Child of the 1980's that I am; I have **MASSIVE** Issues with Females who Believe the Lie: such things are *only* for Impossible Bodies.

But I'm into Chips-Dips-Chains-and-Whips; what does this have to do with the Lifestyle? One nod towards Pony Play or Pet Play tells *THAT* Tale;

sometimes Being Human is the *last* thing the Submissive wants. Dismissing those who dress their Dogs and Cats in booties and such, this is the Rule: **ONLY HUMANS may Wear Clothing.**

Now here is where you have to Understand the Dom-sub Relationship; if she does not like Lingerie for whatever Reason/Excuse, it can be Used as a Weapon. For example... let us say that the Female submissive enjoys Being a Pet; dressing her in Lingerie then becomes a Form of Punishment, reminding her of the Humanity she seeks to escape.

What does this have to do with Shadowrunning? Chummers... *where do you expect to find out about such Things... if* **NOT** *the Shadows?*

Pimpology 101

Pimps **do** Know and Understand the Concept of True Love; it's one of the things that will Fuck with m'Money; you'd better damn well believe a Pimp is able to Spot Love, *especially* when it tries to fuck with Pimp-Thought (the Emotional substitute).

As the **Prime Rule** goes: <u>***Rain, Sleet or Snow, NEVER LOVE NO HO... and the bitch hetter have m'Money.***</u>

* * * *

Treat Females as they want to be treated:

Act like a Lady, Treat her like a Lady.

She wanna be a Silly Ho... hey, that's on her.

Here's the real snag: **WOMEN.**

See... **WOMEN** exist *only* at Age 29 and beyond; below that, there's a belief in this Lie: **I don't Need no Man!!!**

If you can *find* a Real Man at Twenty-Something, lock his ass **DOWN!!** Typically, though, Dogs, Playas, Hustlers, Bad Boys and Wannabes are your Selection this, and nearly every, Evening. A **WOMAN** Understands the Truth: if you are willing to give me what I Need because of Love, fine; everything else is Bullshit or a Hustle and if I don't wanna deal with it I won't. EOF... or Choose Your Death/Jail Sentence, cobber.

* * * *

STREET Pimp Lore says: never trust no Female.

True Pimps Understand: **all** Pimps are paranoid, distrustful fucks; the Bottom Bitch Understand *this:* **Daddy's In a Mood; please Stand By.**

Minority Goth - The Journey and Philosophy of One Black Man

The problem with this Understanding is that the Bottom Bitch is rapidly making the Transition: Ho-to-Wife; if the Pimp ain't ready, he'd better Deal with shit Here/Now.

* * * *

Pimps do not hit Women. Ever; a **WOMAN** is deserving of Respect.

Silly Hoes, Stupid Bitches... **completely different THING**; they tend to be disrespectful in general, and occasionally won't stop *until* someone knocks Fire from their rampaging asses.

* * * *

Wanna Know Why Pimpin' ain't Easy?

You Make Your Money by chasin' lying Hoes who don't get to see Dime Damn ONE from the Efforts of **their** labor, pardon the sick pun; start there, since the whole Legal Side of things is actually a Known Datum. Just ask your Teenage Thug on the Corner; he'll probably fill you in on the Details.

* * * *

Can a Pimp have a Wife? SURE!!

Can a Pimp have an Ol' Lady, as Defined by the Clan Cursed?

Only so long as the Ol' Lady understands the Translation: Love ain't got **SHIT** to do with the Money. By being *Ol' Lady* you have agreed that Clean Pussy and **all** of the Money ***COMES HOME FIRST*** before anything.

* * * *

The only way any Male can Survive Love is to first be a Pimp; a Pimp takes care of Self **FIRST!!** Once that is Settled or at least understood, only then can the Male hope to withstand Love's awesome Might and insidious assaults.

* * * *

The hardest thing for any Pimp, as well as any Hustler or Baller, is the Moment when he reaches Love's Crossroads; Live long enough and you will inevitably encounter this Place. Here, Emotions take the Number one Spot; Money takes Number Two, and to the afore Mentioned Parties, this is an anathema and conundrum. However, it is **WISEST** to take all Lessons Learned from the Past, for they will Apply, in Part or Whole, to the whole Love/Emotions shit pile.

It helps immensely if the Relationship has the **We-Factor**; then shit becomes Standardized: **we** make this Money... **we** Take Care of the **HOME...** etc.

And **NEVER** Forget this: the **GAME NEVER CHANGES, just the Players and them Zeroes on**

the Check, chummer; with Love, you Risk your Emotions instead of/along **with** the Money.

* * * *

Pimp Attrite has changed drastically; only in the Mega-Sprawls (N.Y, Chi-Town, The Big Sleazy, Hotlanta, H-Town, the City of Lost Angels... to name the Major Players in America) is one likely to find a Seventies Exploitation Pimp or something approaching individuality.

There is another Pimp Dress Code, and it terrifies Normal America because of the other Phrases used to Describe it:

Corp Casual. Black Urban Professional doing the Throwback Thing.

Minority Goth.

Smiling Joe Average, U.S.A.

Why the Terror? **You can LIVE next door to this Pimp, have a nice barbecue with him**; he can play Catch with your kids and be a Pillar of the Community...

Runnin' Hoes like it is Blood and Breath and it may well be.

See... a **REAL PIMP** has a certain Hardness to his Gaze, Soul and Aura; no matter how Ancient he gets a **HO** will Respond a certain way, and a Woman... another. That said, clothes do **NOT** make the Pimp...

THE SOUL is PIMP or Punk Bitch Pretender... **EOF.**

* * * *

Pimpology 102

This is the Advanced Class because it Deals with a Pimp's Emotions.

ALL Pimps have Emotions; this is because a True Pimp is a **REAL MAN** First and foremost. True Pimps reserve the Pimp Hand for Bitches, Hoes, and Moments of Ho or Bitch Actions; **never hit a WOMAN!!**

With that out of the way, there may come a Time when the Pimp wants to Leave the Pimp-Game in favor of a Loving Relationship; Understand this First: **a PIMP is a Pimp even after Death and beyond.** Falling in Love, getting Married, even having Children does **not** change or Alter this Basic Truth; the best Outcome possible is to be a man with Pimp *Tendencies*, and even then, you might find many consider you a Hard Man.

* * * *

Separate Emotions from Money; a Pimp **KNOWS** this so long as he's In the Game; step into a Relationship and this gets to be very difficult, but **not** Impossible, to accomplish.

And once done, Trust will come up; this is How to Deal with it:

"Love is one thing; I Trust ONLY **ME** with m'Money."

SHARED Money goes towards the Home, and anything that you **both** Require.

Of course, in a Relationship such as this, **she has Her Money.**

This will Annoy your Pimp Soul, because *any* Female with Money will act Stupid is Pimp Lesson One, Sub-Section Two; the **MAN** Understands that *some* stupidity is actually Human Flavoring. **SOME...** too much must be Dealt with.

A **WOMAN** also Understands these things; Hoes, Bitches and other ne'er do wells either will not or cannot.

* * * *

Money Secured, now comes the **really** Priceless Treasure: your Emotions. All Pimps have them, and Guard them savagely; in a Relationship, your Ol' Lady has this curious Duty: be the Dumping Ground for *some* of your Emotional baggage. It is a Role you share with her; as such, better have Broad Shoulders and a solid Knowledge of where you're dumping your shit.

* * * *

EVERY Pimp should Understand this: Love doesn't Play by any Rules other than its own set of Chaos-crafted bullshit; that said... be Ready for *anything.*

* * * *

Pussy is exactly like Money: shit Comes and Goes all **too** easily; Mind Both and you'll prosper; let one or the other or **both** Rule you... and you'll end up a ruined thing.

* * * *

Pimps do not Fear Love; they simply Understand the Risks involved and make Pimp Decisions based upon the Risks as well as all Risk Assessments.

* * * *

Where Love is concerned... there will come a Crossroads; here a Pimp **will** become utterly confused by their Actions. This is Normal.

Take a step back; avoid all physical contact with **FEMALES**.

Minority Goth - The Journey and Philosophy

of One Black Man

The *instant* you Feel your Thoughts return to Pimp-Centered, Examine your Actions as a Pimp would see shit; if you see Bitch-Ass Nigga... you're Too Close.

Twin Sight

Let me share My New Orleans.

The Big Sleazy, chummers!!!

* * * *

Many Nights began at a one of the many Famous/Infamous Street Corners: this one... historic Bourbon and Bienville. And before you start on Mardi Gras this is Mundane Every Day, not even a Weekend. Just pick a Time and Place... **but *always* stop by during a clear night with just enough breeze to refresh the Sprawl Funk and keep it Moving two miles faster than shit flows downhill.**

And don't start up with the Hoochie Bars and Tourist Traps; I never did. I never visited any Tourist Spot for more than Send-Home Trinkets I never purchased and the Hoochie Bars were Biz **ONLY**, chummers.

See... the Good Little Silas who left Necropolis had to Do Dirt in order to Scrape By at times, something Mom hoped I never had to do but between her and the others I was raised by, Nothing New under Heaven and Earth, cobbers.

Eyes sharp: cop; I ignore him since he's looking at lips. Probably caught someone making the Give-Away Joint Smoking symbol with their hands again and true to the Racist Divide within the Crescent City, I **don't** look for a Black Male... but some College kid being drunk-and-stupid, **EASY PREY** for NOPD.

I hook up with a few of the other Cooks; we Tourist Watch, occasionally bullshitting with a few... cat-calls to drunk Brides-to-be... not many of them tonight; **long** since time past when the Regular Working strippers are indoors, so the ones I spot are Hard Core and serious Money Makers or Hoes makin' their way into the Safe House for the evening...

Should be good Cash floatin' around... time to scrounge up some.

* * * *

Runner: go back and forth from A-to-B. **Today they call him The Transporter... OR DUFFLE BAG BOY!!!!!!!!** Today... this was Years ago, chummer, and I **won't** some kid...

Minority Goth - The Journey and Philosophy

of One Black Man

I was Just another Cook... and **all** Cooks carried backpacks and moved through the Sprawl; wasn't Runnin', it was Day-to-Day in the Big Easy.

So if a Stripper needed coke I ran; from Point a to Point b... <u>***no questions asked... no Names Known.***</u> You Knew Who I was and What I was there for and I made it a point to **never** disturb the Money Flow of any establishment; I Made My Rounds as usual, greeting VIPs sometimes, but **always** Nameless Entities; they had faces, but between the tits and Pussy-covering perfume/cigars... not to mention Lo-Lit Décor...

So the odd looking Black Man frequenting the strip clubs in a duster really **was** a Goth black guy with a Jones for Strippers, <u>***just like everyone else in the Big Sleazy it seemed... NOTHING NEW HERE. NEXT.***</u> Even better... I was **nice** and Friendly... <u>***POLITE AND SOUTHERN GENTEEL WITH just ENOUGH SPRAWL EDGE...***</u>

Occasionally I Ran Blocker: Body Guard for Models on Night Shoots; never bothered me to Skate the Law Considering Necropolis is *notorious* for its Bootlegger and Moonshine Runner: the infamous **Ridge Runners - the beginning of NASCAR!!!**

Tonight is Special; hearing one of the many Illegal Tales...

She ran away from home... came to the Big Sleazy with a solid fake ID and a Dream: to be a Sexy Stripper Girl. Nice Fantasy; the **reality...** nowhere within Spittin' Distance of the **LIE** of Nice. Daddy tracks her to a sleazy club and the cops have to pull the guy off the pavement. No one knows who kicked his ass...

BUT... if ya step down into one of the Hoochie bars you *might* find a Door Man who happens to remember someone scuffed up a bit... some College kid; of course... tucked away in a bathroom ***somewhere*** in the Maze unseen, one of the Pimps who was checkin' up on a troublesome Ho just happened to be there when the shit went down. Between the warrants and the bartender/**SECRET OWNER...**

Need Extraction?

I Ran the Shadows...

* * * *

And then... Necropolis:

First major Night Difference, other than the Lights, Sprawlless Nature-plus-City-in-Training crispness... ***NO MUSIC!!!!!!!!!!!!!!!!!!!***

They like it *quiet* at Night; easier to hear someone sneakin' up on ya.

Minority Goth - The Journey and Philosophy

of One Black Man

Yeah... **FEAR** runs Necropolis; did when I was a kid; will run the joint well beyond **my** rotting corpse.

Then there are the Head Games; with little to Distract you save drinking to excess and fuckin' everything that'll hold still for a nano-tick, there are No Activities for the Mind; actually rather **shunned** upon, those things. The Farmer's Mentality stuck here, and for some Reason, ignorance-is-Bliss or Bust became the unofficial Motto. And you'd better not buck the System with **IDEAS!!!!!!!!!!**

Just drop off the money and leave us in peace.

Head Games became something **FAMILIES** specialized in...

Blood Traits...

So. There is Country Music. There is Rap. There is Gospel. If it is Canned Music, done-and-done again; Popular Culture? **SURE...**; we filter that out with the other 486 Channels of absolute White Noise we call Cable/Dish Television. Please note the **OFF Switch.**

Thing is, this is the place where, according to **OUTSIDE NECROPOLIS LORE/LEGEND**, you find the Classic Good Southern Genteel Woman... Angel on Earth... **a Perfect Image**; And you can **easily and RIGHTLY** add any and every non-White stereotype; Necropolis is the **PLACE** where such

Females sprout up and it ain't necessarily Fun-Happy all of the time.

But to get **THOSE** Tales... Gotta be In-the-Loop.

GOTTA RUN DIFFERENT SHADOWS...

Wanna Know Power in Necropolis? **KEEP Secrets.** Be the Joker who won't tell a Soul shit and you'll quickly discover just how much Power... **and terror...** you Generate.

As for my part, Stand-offish... so I shouldn't KNOW anyone or anything.

Except for those few Here/Now Hard and Legendary O.G.s and other Fresh Homes (released from **Penitentiary Stays... not just the Local Jail they** *still* **have with the Town Drunk!!!**); they give me Street Cred and Respect that many Locals do not like... **especially** considering I don't **dress like them!!!!!!!!!!!!**

I ain't Normal; that makes me Dangerous... a THREAT!!!!

So they look to their Females, wondering what Evils I have in store for them. Why?

Isn't that what Hollywood SEZ happens next?

Entertainment?

Country Boy Bored, chica, Race-be-damned; so you can *expect* those Long Nights sitting along, staring at the stars over a set of train tracks. **SURE** you can bring your Smart Phone for your tunes; gonna bring **mine** and a six-pack... maybe holla at this guy I know... works with a Cook... *you know they **always** have Good Pot; I hear it comes with the job.*

Rich Kid? Fire off a few texts and there'll be a Drug Drop at school come tomorrow, and MILFY will pitch an unholy fit if Junior fucks her (in return for **not** telling his dad about the sack he forgot about in his pants that day... **son is now Mommy's Dealer!!!**)

Rich Kid... Poor Black Kid from Da Hood; both Duffle Bag Boys; Same Shit... Different Toilet, chummers. Most people in the Big Sleazy Know and Understand this: they **say** it in Necropolis, but still believe their shit doesn't stink and it's someone else's Responsibility to keep the Crapper Clean.

It's where they do their Deep Thinking...; I say ***look at the Fraggin Results chummer: A FRESH PILE OF FERTILIZER!!!!!!!!!***

* * * *

Overly Romantic View of the Big Easy? Yep.

Because for me Romance is **HARD**; the Big Easy helped me See this clearly, revealing the Truth of something I came up with in Necropolis' Sister Sprawl the CDZ:

In All Things... Balance... THIS is the First Form.

Flowers and Fancy Dinners... Check; for me, the Rose must come with Thorns.

In the Big Sleazy... ***CHECK.***

Here in Necropolis, being in the Lifestyle terrifies **everyone!!!!!!** Race is one Reason, since **everyone** sez only White Females are into Bondage (gotta ask a Local for the Specific Rule and other identifying markers; gotta be someone On the Books... everything *else* is... or isn't...) and that means interracial Sex, Domestic abuse, the cops (**never a Loving Relationship within the Lifestyle... impossible.**); the other is that I **came** from here; *that* means such Ideas **can and DO** come from this Pristine American Double Standard Poster Child-Village Societal Experiment, mutated beyond its meager Comprehension.

They experience... yet do not Comprehend:

The Shadows are Evolving...

Now, Parent's Worst Fears some Twenty Years ago; Sci-Fi Horror of the Machine running our Lives...

Chummer... we **are** Borg; pick your mindset:

Big Easy: Dress up occasionally and LAUGH **at yourself...**

Necropolis: *Cower in Fear of **ALL** Dark Thoughts within you, pray hard. Go to Church Every Sunday and talk about your neighbor, cause he sure is runnin' **his** mouth about your shit!!!* **Just remember to ALWAYS LOOK Your Best when you ass-fuck him over;** <u>***Appearances First. Always.***</u>

Seated on the Throne of Bones

From the Soul of

The Hood Born Dom

Observations of a Hood Born Dom

I remember this Moment:

She had said something about light bondage. At the Time, it was a simple curiosity. So... we talked about it... and thus the Situation: me spanking her.

I Remember... because it felt Right and Proper to assume a Role... that of the Stern yet Caring Hand.

I also Remember being pissed when she stopped. Not because she stopped me, but because of the Why Behind:

"I was about to cum... didn't want to."

I was upset... and my first Thought: ***SO!?!?! LET ME FINISH!!***

I do not like being disturbed when I am Under.

* * * *

The best way to accept Denial is to understand the Why Behind.

This is **best**; it is seldom easy.

* * * *

There are many who want unchecked, Unconditional Love.

Fine.

BE ETERNALLY LOYAL AND FAITHFUL... EVEN BEYOND DEATH.

* * * *

I never understood Flirting.

Lies coated with Honey... believed blindly... and for what? Sex... pure and simple. Temporary... what... Comfort? Affection?

If Love is sought, better to seek... elsewhere.

I **Know** it is **supposed** to make the other participant feel good about themselves.

Always figured **that** should be done well in advance.

I do Understand that Being Honest often surprises... if not offends.

This puzzles me.

* * * *

When I was a kid someone said, *"Ugly people need Love too!"*

I believe everyone needs Love; it's the **Definition** that tends to cause issues.

* * * *

This is the Theory of Panties:

Granny Panties: Highly Conservative; definitely Vanilla.

¾ Panties: Normal Female

Bikini Briefs: Normal with a bit more Wild.

T-Back Thong: Wild Streak

Thong: Slut

This Theory is Modified by Stylistic Demands. **Always**.

Then there is this... need... to Feel Sexy. Internally or for someone; I often wonder which but only for a Moment.

In the end, Panties make a Female feel... Human.

Be Mindful of this Truth.

* * * *

Let me Discuss the Black Man-Big Woman... Thing.

Yes it happens... **often**.

The basis is best Placed here: way back when, a big Woman was considered healthy. It stuck.

That is an Excuse.

* * * *

I watched a Woman go Under; she was submissive.

For her... it was a joyous Occasion.

For me... it was a savage, unholy beautiful, powerful Moment... one that terrified me to no end.

Why?

Because *I* was the Reason she was there.

I had never considered it: Taking a Woman that far... ever.

It was easy, and easy caused me unnerving paranoia... rampant Fear.

* * * *

At Work there are Times when I let the cold Professional Asshole fade... and allow everyone to see/See me when I am not in the Kitchen.

Some approach timidly. Others examine me with judgmental glances semi-secretively slid towards me.

For those I speak freely and easily with, there is this to say: they wait for it now; there is little Fear in their eyes.

There **is**, however, the prepared steel when one knows they are going to be shocked by something.

* * * *

I don't like tits; I have always been a Thigh Man.

This is probably due to the constant Info-Dump: something lay hidden between a Female's Thighs that I, as a Male, should Covet.

So I find it amusing that nearly every Female alive first considers her Thighs, along with ass and stomach... when Thoughts of Being Fat enter the Equation.

I have never considered weight, just what is visually appealing.

Minority Goth - The Journey and Philosophy

of One Black Man

* * * *

I Remember my first Thought after my first orgasm within a female... condom covered, for the nosey:

*Well... **THAT'S** over with; what was all the fuss about?*

This is not to say that I did not enjoy myself, only a Reminder that even **then** I Knew there was More.

I also remember our next Round... which started with finger-fucking. I got four into her and after my next orgasm, she quietly asked how many. I told her, but only allowed my Tone to Ask the next Question:

As a female you give birth... right? Baby comes down same tube; head is probably bigger than the fist... certainly wider; what's the deal?

Yes this is Youthful Ignorance on Many Levels. It is also a Moment when Important Questions were never Asked or Answered.

Thus... blundering; be Mindful of this.

* * * *

Things my Mother told me:

If you ever want a black 'woman' to Show her Color, wet her hair.

Don't Count my Money for me.

You look evil. ***{{this was said when I was Thinking}}***

* * * *

Fear and Trust. They are inescapably Connected.

* * * *

I watched a young Woman constantly put on a False Face today. The Why Behind is as puzzling as it is... strange.

Our Relationship is strictly Professional; I've never hung out with her Socially. So any friendly Emotions are confined to the Workplace. Yet it must be stated that she seemed uncomfortable putting that Face on. She even snapped... highly uncharacteristic.

It is Ego to assume I am **the** Why behind; it is prudent to See the Connection.

* * * *

I never found this odd:

Every submissive, who is submissive by Nature, tends to Desire Safety. Regardless of her Suffering or Torment; the sub **NEEDS** to eventually Feel Safe.

Minority Goth - The Journey and Philosophy of One Black Man

It's all too easy to Hurt; being someone the submissive can come to and Know that for the Moment, they are Safe? **THAT** takes Trust on their Part and Balanced Strength, Patience, and more Heart than anyone truly Understands, unless they **are** this Soul.

For them there is a Title: Dom.

* * * *

I never liked the Title *Master*; aside from the whole Racial issue... me being Black and all that goodness... there is the general Concept of Master.

Master holds Life and Death; seemed pathetic. Master is fueled by Power and Anger; seemed Pointless.

As for Titles, I prefer Sir; my Reason is probably personal Stupidity and Defined thusly:

Sir is an Elder. Sir Guides with Wisdom and Knowledge. Sometimes... Sir Punishes, but there is **never** Anger. For Sir, there is always an Endless Love that cannot be adequately Defined and is often mistaken for overly-casual Banter. Sir only Requires Compliance and Acceptance of Consequences/Responsibilities. Sir only Requires Honesty.

In Defining the Title, I aid in my Definition/Reality.

* * * *

This is one Honorable Way to introduce someone to the Fact that you are within the Lifestyle; tell them while eating a nice, relatively quiet lunch. Do not give any details unless you feel they are warranted.

Yet you must always understand: Acceptance is out of your Control; that Power lies with the Listener.

* * * *

My grand-mother told me this:

Never let a woman mark you.

This was told to me after a round of sex with my... well... Girlfriend; she'd dug her nails into my back and left me with a scar I still carry. Yet what I remember most about that Session was the cruel joy in her eyes, and **that** is what makes my grand-mother's words Wise ones.

She has a Way of Knowing a Person's Soul with a glance, a trait I share in Spades times ten.

* * * *

I live in Da Hood... or what will become Da Hood if things progress as I foresee.

In Da Hood there are Hood Rats; these are Females (by virtue of Genetic Selection, **NOT** because of strict Definition) who seem to revel in being Stupid, ignorant, Rude and behaving in any manner guaranteed to offend anyone with a shred of Sensibilities. If this sounds Stereotypical, consider this: being a Hood Rat is **PART** upbringing... part **CHOICE!!!!**

* * * *

When two Black Males pass each other in Da Hood, they Eyeball each other.

This is blatant animalistic Instinct... and Street Law. Unless you have zero intention of Starting Shit, the best option is to meet the gaze evenly **WHILE IN THE PROCESS OF EXAMINING YOUR SURROUNDINGS WITH CASUAL EASE. UNDER NO CIRCUMSTANCE SHOULD YOUR EYES OR BODY LANGUAGE SHOW FEAR.**

* * * *

This is a Street Axiom I have Personal Experience with... somewhat:

Can't turn a Ho into a Housewife.

The Why Behind is simplistic: Mindset. The Mindsets of a *Ho* and *Housewife* are completely at odds with each other.

* * * *

This is an unfortunate Truth in the South and probably elsewhere as well:

A Black Male Dom with a White Female sub is not Lifestyle; it is Domestic Violence.

Be Mindful of this if you ever have need of the Police in your Home.

* * * *

Just because a thing is True does **NOT** make it Right.

This is a matter where Word Definition is Key.

* * * *

This is Cypher:

Puff, Puff, Pass to the left.

Don't break Rotation.

Don't bogart. (baby-sit, hog are acceptable)

This is disheartening:

There are ten-year-old children who know this and have experienced it First-hand.

I was thirteen when I came to Know Cypher. I was thirty-two when I came to Know the disheartening Truth with frightening clarity.

* * * *

I remember getting a beating because I called a girl close to my own age a bitch.

I remember being upset (pissed... but I was young) at being punished for telling the Truth: she **was** a bitch.

I Remember my mom's boyfriend backing me up, but not getting in the way of my punishment.

I remember him punishing her in his own way: ignoring her and when he did acknowledge her he brought up the unnecessary punishment.

He would later earn the Title *Father* from me.

* * * *

You will hear these Words countless Times; mark them well for they are a Universal Truth:

Any idiot can make a baby; it takes a Man to be a Father.

* * * *

She held me close and gave me several pecks on the cheeks; the first few were hesitant... but I digress.

I Understand, "I love you," is often tossed about casually.

So. I allow the Lie to pass harmlessly over my Essence.

* * * *

If you ever want the Truth from Your Boy (a Hood Term I shall Define later), buy **one round** of beer. Never a mixed drink or cocktail... Beer. Select a bar they feel comfortable in, but do not run rough-shod in.

* * * *

I don't Dazzle for dick.

When a Female flaunts her hair, tits, ass, whatever, I look to slot the dimensions and movements into Memory but I don't get lost in, "... those tits!!!"; instead I lock gazes.

Now... it has been said I have an intimidating presence. So it stands to Reason that **IF** this is True, then my gaze is equally intimidating.

Thus... Fear in eyes should be expected.

So too should submission be Expected.

* * * *

Dazzle distracts; that is its **only** Purpose/Reason.

Dazzle prevents forward Movement; Dazzle inhibits Growth.

Dazzle hides Lies **and** Truth.

* * * *

There are common Excuses for an impromptu Social Gathering; alcohol and drugs are common and share this:

They inhibit Control.

Be Mindful of this. **Always**.

* * * *

This is the Foundation of the Rabbit Hole Theory:

Sex is a Physical Act; it brings Physical Pleasure.

The Rest is Human; emotions and such fall into this Category.

* * * *

People Fear what they do not Understand.

So to say she Understands me is a lie; she is not Aware of every Dark Thought... every Twisted Notion.

Fear becomes Seductive when there is the possibility/lie/hope of Learning more if one endures.

Yet one thing must **never** be forgotten: you never know Everything.

THIS is true Understanding.

* * * *

I don't Ho Hop; that is... I don't stick dick into any willing Hole.

I don't have Game.

This is Street... the darkest Shadows; ***True Players ain't got Game; true Players don't Play.***

To others this Means that even when I am not looking for something, I am Looking. I see much more than I let on; always have.

This frightens Hoes. It also frightens Sheep.

Yet Women may find this Addictive.

* * * *

This is a Kitchen Hook-Up Flow:

Drinks/smoke after Work... to blow off steam/relax.

Location doesn't matter; if the **goal** is to get mindfragged and Sex is a possibility, this is Hook-Up.

It is also dangerous.

* * * *

Minority Goth - The Journey and Philosophy of One Black Man

This Event happened to me:

I am not accustomed to being hit on, so when it happens I Notice. There are two Females vying for my attention... one with a definite, and highly visible, lead. She quietly spoke of Matters pertaining to the other suitor.

This jockeying for position is Normal.

Be mindful of subterfuge and deceit in such Matters.

* * * *

The Streets; it is a living Entity, regardless of the physical Location.

All Streets seethe with barely controlled Rage; calling it anger implies the Creature with the Emotion is Human... and such is not always the Case.

* * * *

It helps to Feel Good and Confident within your clothes.

* * * *

Watch out for Gold Diggers. Spotting one is difficult at times. However... once you hear them Speak it becomes easy to Hear the Sound of Dollar Signs in her Careless Whispers.

* * * *

Cock Blocking: the act of disturbing someone's attempt to get laid/Hook Up with another person.

In the Streets only your Friend can safely Cock Block a Brotha; safely being a Relative Term.

* * * *

The hardest Thing I have had to deal with as a Black Dom is my selection for Dating Material; I tend to prefer Non-African-American Females.

I could craft libraries on the Why Behind, however this is not about the Why Behind... but the easy Lie everyone sees: a Black Man abusing his White Lover. Being raised in the South I understand the Lie; what I do not Understand is Why they make the connection **after** being told the Nature of the Relationship.

In the end, I tire myself out in my attempt to See Logic in blind, racist, Bible-fed Southern Mentality.

* * * *

The Human Body is Hard Wired for Self-Correction; so it comes as little surprise that after the Body experiences Pain, it doses itself with What-Me-Worry. This is the beginning of the Addictive Quality found within every Pain Slut.

* * * *

Recently I was Reminded of this: Age does not Matter where Likes/Dislikes are concerned. That said, do not be surprised or shocked or repulsed by a grandmother/grandfather within the Lifestyle; **Never underestimate the Depths of Human Depravity.**

* * * *

Mathematics

I don't get it.

While shooting the shit with a guy about one of his conquests... one I knew some, but not a great deal, about... I mentioned something Personal about his Conquest.

He seemed surprised to hear of this. Never mind he'd fucked her many times.

HOW CAN YOU FUCK SOMEONE AND NOT KNOW SQUAT ABOUT THEM?

The only possible Answer is the Definition of Fucking: ones partner is not considered Human; therefore nothing Human (emotions, personality, etc.) enters into the Equation.

* * * *

No Relationship is ever 1+1; others will add in their worth/worthlessness and some may seek to subtract from what is there already.

* * * *

In the Streets, Terminology is important to Understand.

* * * *

If your Ol' Lady or Girl flips out, looses her mind, or in any other way goes off on you there are several Reactions possible.

However it must be Understood that there are only two Reactions that have any real Guarantee. Leaving her guarantees no violence then and there; hitting her guarantees you Drama... which may well include you losing your Freedom.

* * * *

It's always good to know something about a Female's Friends and Associates... if only to have passing knowledge with a possible Source for bullshit.

* * * *

Every Dom should watch, but not get involved with, a Relationship breaking down. In fact... several; this is because it is always best to familiarize ones

Mind with just how Shit Happens, as this Event will fuck up any equation, guaranteed.

* * * *

There are two types of submissives: strong and weak.

A weak submissive will inevitably become a Psycho Bitch... utterly self-destructive.

A strong submissive is rare and can only be found within the Soul of a Woman.

* * * *

It is rare to find an African-American Female submissive.

Hood Rats are like pennies: plenty of them and they tend to be easily tossed aside and not missed.

Gold Diggers flock to money; Sharks want money **and** power.

* * * *

The most annoying part of being a Hood-raised Dom is dealing with perception.

In the Streets there is little Street-difference between a Dom and a Pimp/Playa.

* * * *

One difference between a Dom and a Playa is similar to the difference between Truth and Lie.

* * * *

I Give only what I am Given.

Given kindness and compassion... I return them.

Given anything negative... I return that.

In this there is Honor; in the Streets this makes me an Angry Black Man.

* * * *

Whenever a Black Female sweetens her Tone I get Angry; they **ALWAYS** want something and have zero intention of compensating me for my Time/Effort.

However... occasionally there are Searching Tones to such requests. These are looking for Anger... for they Fear it.

I look for this because in Searching they may Find something else.

* * * *

I have Sadistic tendencies; thus it helps to look for Females who enjoy receiving Pain from Loving Hands.

If this sounds impossible, then I can honestly say you have never encountered a true Pain Slut.

Conflict of Interest

I have only Fucked one Ho and she was a Crack Ho. How it came to be was a Matter of T-Monkey Bonding in the Big Sleazy. It was my only such occurrence and one I wish to never repeat. This is Why:

Hoes don't have a Soul. Hoes are Tools only.

I prefer Women. Women have Souls.

* * * *

I had a Co-Worker look at me as if I were somewhat unstable mentally.

It is interesting to Note that they only looked at me this way when they saw the Master's Expressions.

* * * *

It is wise to listen to gossip, especially from a Female who makes it a point to be nosey.

The wisdom comes from this: even if the Data is all False it is good to know where the Data comes from; often, the Why Behind the Data Stream fed from that Source tells a larger Tale.

* * * *

When considering Paying for Sex... consider this:

The Street Axiom is very True: *you **always** Pay for Sex*.

This is where Humanity differs from Logic: Humanity considers payment to mean monetary compensation only.

Logic dictates that Payment takes any Form within Humanity's Arsenal.

So it should come as no surprise that Logic here is Cold and impersonal.

* * * *

Where I Live... and in most of the Places I've dossed-down... you are not considered a Man unless you **actively** cheat or have cheated. Then you are considered less than a Man if you cannot **stop** cheating. And if you **have** cheated you are **expected** to cheat again.

Net sum: ***there is no Trust in the Definition of Man.***

I would Change this.

* * * *

In New Orleans I was told this with regards to dating so-called Black Women: ***you can't be afraid to bat 'em up.***

Yes this is Domestic Violence; unless you understand one key Dynamic within the Stereotypical Black Male-Black Female Street/Sprawl/Hood Relationship: ***IF IT'S NEGATIVE... IT'S EXPECTED***.

Then it becomes a sad Tradition.

* * * *

I ponder this often:

Some Need to hear Words of Affection. Yet when Real Actions backing them up are offered, the Action is often looked at with Double Vision as an attempt is made to see the 'real' Reason behind said Action.

This is Strange to me.

* * * *

I have been a Pimp; certain Lessons stick.

Like making eye contact with a Hoe; unless it's Biz... don't.

Now some Females have Hoe Tendencies; making eye contact with a Female with Hoe Tendencies is dangerous... as the contact is often mistaken for Interest.

* * * *

You can always tell when you're in the Presence of a Woman:

You don't Run Game; you Come Real, or sit on the sidelines and Dream.

You smile, pull yourself up to full height... ***and adjust your clothing and general Appearance!!! Sloppy will not do***.

You can always spot a Real Woman when, after doing these things, she addresses you as a Human Being. Friendly Banter or Honest Emotion... she Responds as a Human and addresses you as a Human.

* * * *

I have been a Pimp; Pimpin' **ain't** Easy.

The Saying, "It takes a Real Man to be a Pimp."... isn't quite True.

Minority Goth - The Journey and Philosophy of One Black Man

It takes a Hard Man to be a successful Pimp.

The trouble with being Hard all the damn time is that there is no Balance Within.

* * * *

There is one Female who Distracts me.

I recently saw her in Street Casual... her own Style.

I cannot remember the blouse... only that it fit perfectly.

I remember the pants because of her ass... I like asses.

But what I will never Forget... is her Presence. Clothed as her Heart Dictated, there was a Light that utterly blinded even my deepest Sight.

Beautiful Women **DO** Exist.

* * * *

There is Power in giving someone a Nickname. There is a Human Connection in giving someone a Nickname.

Therefore, it should come as no surprise that when I give one it is Earned.

If I do not... there are Reasons.

* * * *

I was in a Relationship that had this Comment... often: *you two finish each other's sentences.*

It was Natural to me.

This was due to the Fact that I made an Effort to Know and Understand my Significant Other.

* * * *

Cash... grass... ass; no one Rides for Free.

I learned this back in the Seventies... early eighties; it still holds True.

* * * *

I don't do Drunk Girls; and yes... once drunk... all Females become Girls.

Now Stoner Chics... yes... I will and have done.

There is no Real Difference; mindfragged is mindfragged.

However... every Stoner Chic I've ever come across has a way of studying the guys around them. Sure it's mostly for Sexual Purposes... but the Focus is different... more intense.

Drunk... there is no control.

This is a Personal Preference.

Minority Goth - The Journey and Philosophy of One Black Man

* * * *

Hood raised Females... regardless of Color... have certain expectations sexually. They also tend to reinforce these expectations amongst their Social Groups.

Chief among these is Size. Another... is forcefulness; mark my Word Choice well.

And without fail the Man is an after-thought... if he is Thought of at all.

* * * *

Get to Know me before you end up with my Dick in your mouth and my balls on your chin; seems like Common Sense to me.

But I can never speak those Thoughts... ever; too Rude... crass... and **HONEST**.

Besides... the accepted Method is get her drunk.

No; this marks me as a Guy looking for a Wife.

It never ceases to confound me; where does this Logic Flow come from? I **KNOW** it is Stupid... but where does it come from?

When I make the effort to Get to Know a Female it is **assumed** that I want Sex. And if I do not... then **that** is considered a Rejection... and I'm playing with her.

YOU CANNOT BE HONEST TO A FEMALE.

You can lie... with a shitload of Please-See-Addendum Loophole Bull.

But you cannot be Honest.

Especially if they ask for it.

If they demand it... you can do a 50/50 mix... but nothing more.

I don't like those Rules and do not Play that game; all or nothing.

Risky... sure; where is the joy in Safety?

I Know where the Pain will come... and Prepare for it; I cannot prevent it.

That is Life; I Deal as best I can given the shit-pile I have.

Get to Know Me; and stop looking at the Style of Dress.

THAT is designed to Cloak in Shadows... and does its job well.

The Truth... as always... lies Within.

And it pays to get to Know the idiot you're about to bump uglies with.

Minority Goth - The Journey and Philosophy

of One Black Man

Thoughts of a Hood-Born Dom

Here is the problem with being this person: **someone to Talk to**.

Aside from being **a** Vault of someone else's Secrets/Lies/Words... there may well come a Moment when Talk is not the Why Behind.

From a head-nod-and-bob-Yes-Man to... well... Backdoor Lover; every Drama drenched scenario Exists with Being Someone to Talk To.

And yet... for there to be Trust in any Relationship it is a Position one must Master.

* * * *

It is difficult to Define ones Essence... only if one insists on Being Blind.

The only Place to Find ones Essence is on the other side of Adversity/Challenge.

Once Defined there is either Acceptance or Denial.

* * * *

I often Ponder on this:

Most submissives have a temper. Most tend to hide their submissive Nature in Public and grow frustrated in one Manner or another.

I wonder Why they seek Quiet Doms in loud Places... Places where Frustration is almost guaranteed.

* * * *

This often happens:

Black Women, raised in Da Hood, are often taught to never put too much faith... and zero Trust... **in Males**.

Which leaves Pleasure to Matters of the Flesh; you cannot find Pleasure in a walk along the beach with someone you do not Trust.

* * * *

I wrestled a Young Lady. In the End, it was a form of Foreplay... but it was never just that.

Aside from arousing both of us... I found that I saw through the Lie of our action.

Turn her on... but she never really wanted to Win. She tried to escape... this was True; yet in the end... there was always a Look in her Eyes.

Not Defeat... submission; and before **that**... there would be the Waiting.

She would wait for me to gloat... show some Sign of my Triumph.

This Separates me from what is 'known' about Doms:

Until she Yielded the Struggle would Continue. Once she Yielded, she was Mine; My Will held Sway. Sure she'd get dick; I wanted pussy.

But... I would Tinker first.

She knew... and experienced several Good and Poor Moments during my Tinkering.

We both learned; I Grew.

The End was Known; why gloat when there was Work to be done?

* * * *

Never say, "I told you so." It serves no Purpose... not even Torment/Pain/Humiliation.

It only births Guilt in their Thoughts.

And Guilt breeds Doubt.

* * * *

"A Slut will do anything."

I remember hearing that as a kid... and letting my youthful imagination go wild.

As I grew up I came to Understand the Lie of those Words... and the Truth of a Slut.

In the Definition... there **are** Limits.

Known... and yes... Dark... **but Limits Exist**.

Be Mindful of this.

* * * *

I am paranoid. That said... it is Natural that I watch everything around me.

I learned to hide my paranoia with practiced, easy Glances, and honed my Memory to Burn images into Place.

I am an Honest, Honorable Man. That said... it is Natural for others to be afraid.

Honest Men are rare... and Dangerous.

The combination is unsettling to look at; I appear to be... Serious.

This bothers those accustomed to Easy Lies and False Happiness because what I See differs from what they see.

* * * *

Minority Goth - The Journey and Philosophy of One Black Man

There are Times when being a Dom gets in the way. This typically happens when I have to be the Social Dom. Think Washington Lackey that happens to be somewhat likeable; fits... since I have worked there.

What I find peculiar... is how a submissive Female will react when I do this; without fail... they snarl.

Peculiar... and amusing; they seem to Know the Wrongness of the Face and Tone. Understanding does not make it any less False.

I smile.

* * * *

I have not encountered a Black Woman submissive. I know they Exist; I have not encountered one. Da Hood doesn't breed submissive Females. Hood Rats, Hoes, Silly Broads... yes; Baby-Makin'-Drama-Machines... too many to count.

And on the off chance she spits the Strong Black Woman rant... there is still the Hope of a Black Female being born.

Black Women are a dead species... unfortunately.

* * * *

I never Understood Racism; still don't.

As was Passed On to me from an Executive Chef... all pussy is Pink on the Inside.

Crude... but damn true. After that it gets to be Individual Preferences... and **THAT** is a big pond to swim.

* * * *

From start to Finish there is a Method to Putting Someone In Their Place.

That said... one should Know their Method as breath.

In Knowing the Method you also Know others; they Follow where you Lead.

* * * *

Let us discuss Restraints.

I do not care what the chosen Method is... the Reason for Restraint is the same: **it is the Reason the submissive Knows, Believes and Understands within herself...** in this case.

I have no Need for Rope.

I **DO**, however, require a different Method of Restraint.

Free to Move about... dodge... escape... it takes a great deal of Inner Restraint to simply stand there and Experience Pleasure/Pain.

And should she Need Restraints?

Fine; Learn how to do so Properly. Experiment within Limits; these things are Known to Doms.

In the End... For this particular Dom, **her Needs are met: EOF**.

* * * *

I have no Need for Rope.

What I Require, however, is difficult.

I Require Control; for many... this is unacceptable. Even though I do not Require Direct Control, they find it unacceptable.

These are Chaos Spawn. Drama Queens. Hood Rats. Gossip Whores; the list of names is endless. One I find best: *Useless*.

* * * *

I am not sure of this:

Every submissive I have ever known... Needs to be useful. They Need to Exist for a Reason... and most... Need this from **just one Soul**.

I Know there is Truth here...

* * * *

I Know what I can Control.

I **Know** what I cannot Control.

With Control... I have Ways... My Way.

Without Control... I simply don't give a shit until it crashes my universe... **then** I Seize Control.

* * * *

Speak Honestly to a Black Female... and if she's Hood-Raised, but not a Hood Rat... here is what will happen:

She will recoil... and not speak for several months. However... she will watch you... and if your Words match your Actions... she will **eventually** speak occasionally.

She has accepted you... somewhat; be Mindful of this.

* * * *

In the South... once you are of Legal Age it is considered Robbing-the-Cradle **IF and ONLY IF** the Age Difference is eight or more years.

At Seven... they start counting Months.

This is for the Purpose of Gossip.

Minority Goth - The Journey and Philosophy

of One Black Man

* * * *

Here's a very mean Trick:

If you **ever** want a black Female to Show-her-Color... get her hair wet.

This was told to me by my Mother.

* * * *

I have seen submissive Females who often have the I-Can-Change-Him-With-Good-Lovin' Look in their eyes.

This is Doomed from the Moment it becomes even Thought's shadow.

* * * *

I don't like tits; they are distracting.

Some Females are proud of their tits... and rightly so in some cases.

However... if you would strut them around then bear the burden of my Thoughts.

Tits Exist to mark Feminine Status... feed newborns... and to be Tormented.

Abide by those Rules; **THEN** I will grant any Female the Right to be Proud of those distractions.

* * * *

Hip-Hop and Rap are different... yet they serve a similar Purpose: Warnings.

As usual... no one listens unless it makes Money... so what is Heard is guaranteed slanted.

* * * *

This often happens in Black Communities:

When a Male child is raised by nearly all Females, his Male Influences are limited to a scattered View of Males via the Female influences... and Images best Worded by the Hip Hop Lyricist *Rakim*:

Raised by Gangster and Gamblers

Hustlers, Con Artists

Convicts, Killers and Dons

Drug Deals, Playas and Pimps

Smooth Talkers

Stick-Up Kids

Thugs

Real Niggas

and Gods

{{From *The R*}}

Minority Goth - The Journey and Philosophy

of One Black Man

Thus... my Quest to Define Being a Man within the Black Community... is necessary. That it **is** Necessary is sad.

* * * *

There is a Stereotype; it is called Angry Black Man.

For some... I fit this... somewhat; this is typical of most Views and the Naked Truth: I do not Fit within any Stereotype precisely.

* * * *

I never learned to Flirt... not according to Street, Da Hood, or any other Social Standard.

I did, however, learn that speaking with Cold, brutal Honesty often frightens a Female... not bring them a smile as I **still** Feel it should. After all... when I tell a Female she is beautiful, I mean it... and it Shows.

Yet without fail... there is Fear in their eyes; it filters into the air... a dangerous Scent on the Wind.

* * * *

The most horrid place to Exist is within Solitude. When even Background Noise ceases to be heard...

when Temperature Differences are all varying levels of imagined Light and Shadow...

Eventually... even Thought ceases to Exist within Solitude.

And if you manage to crawl your way out... you are never the same. Ever.

It is Wise to Accept this... but **never** dwell upon your Stay within Solitude.

* * * *

These are my Definitions:

Ol' Lady: This is the one you Answer to; by this... I mean the Woman you actually take Time to Speak to... and Listen to. With here, there is Conversation and Discussion. Emotions cause Arguments here, but those Rules are well documented... if not Followed.

Girlfriend: This is best said by *Juvenile*: when she starts fuckin' with your nerves, kick her to the curb. All 'dates' end with the Horizontal Shuffle; it never goes beyond Sex.

Wife: You are married to this one; this does **not** mean she is your Ol' Lady. Be mindful of this.

* * * *

I have only hit one Female in my entire Existence.

It taught me that no matter how much I try, there is always something that **can** break a Man's Word.

If Challenged... Face it head on... and do no not worry about failure. Do not worry about Winning... however Defined; Face it with Cold Honesty.

Aside from being an Honorable Way... it tends to work.

* * * *

If you do not Mean it... and are not willing to Suffer for it... ***NEVER SAY, "I Love You."***

* * * *

I have Experienced a Moment of Pure Happiness:

I was sitting in front of my computer 'station' in my doss... puttering; she was behind me... and wrapped her arms around my chest. Her head poked over my right shoulder... and I inhaled her Presence... then Willed every Burden on my Shoulders out of Existence.

This... the calm of that Moment... is what I call a Happy Moment within my Life.

* * * *

When I wear Black... there are Times when I can use the Color... expand it into my aura.

And during those Moments... I Sense Fear from those nearby.

Only now do I See another pattern; those who stand there, drenched in fear... are all submissive in one Way or another.

When I Look Within... I see only Cold, Heartless Control.

* * * *

I Think too much.

If I were to ever have any Experience with a Female for who ropes and Bondage went beyond the physical... I would frustrate her with constant Questions.

Not about the Details of the physical, but because I want to Know something very specific: **what <u>she</u> Experienced, Thought, Knows, Understands**.

That is the True Hard Data... and where Truth resides.

Unfortunately... the Answers require complete Trust.

* * * *

I have used restraints... but never the 'official' style. Always using what was on hand, I now find pleasure in having very little to work with.

Minority Goth - The Journey and Philosophy of One Black Man

I have learned to astound my Other with my Imagination... and the rather cold way Ideas seem to simply pop/Exist within my Mind... and they always search my Face... looking for Clues.

* * * *

There is a saying amongst Males. It's rather recent I believe, though its origins probably date back to the first caveman who got into a fight. While the saying does have an element of violence, it is primarily a sexual performance descriptor. I'll state it in this form:

My Kung Fu is good.

It should be stated that this is only one version; multiple variations exist throughout the globe and cross all barriers. That statement is, in my estimate, American.

This is not an attempt to explain anything; I merely scrip words surrounding that basic statement. That said, some may well be offended. That is their right; personally I don't give a rip.

Within these Tales and Stories and Scribbles I attempt to define this statement as well as put forth my own admittedly twisted View.

{{*Introduction from Techniques*}}

* * * *

It doesn't surprise me that someone used the Lifestyle as **Game Play**; it also doesn't surprise me that it was successful. Pisses me off to no end, but considering what I Know about Playas... not beyond the scope of possibility; in fact it's a wonder I haven't stumbled across it before... and may **have...** though I most likely only saw the destructive ends. That... and I was too young to Understand a damn thing; still and all... now that I've stumbled across this happenstance...

For a submissive Female... this is probably the **NORM!!!!**

The Game don't Change...

Minority Goth Presents:

The Hood Born Dom

I am the Hood Born Dom; I have Hood Ways as a Function of my Upbringing and Experiences. This cannot be helped or altered drastically... and I have **ZERO INTENTION** of doing so. That said, there **is** something to this: every now and again the Hood Nigga crops up; it Serves as a shitty Ego, but sans the Real Deal... it has its Uses at times.

Money First... everything else later. For every Female who believes such a Male cannot Love... try this: **Do You...**

Males... get your Head screwed on straight before **attempting** a Serious Relationship; know your Limits and be ready to redefine them. I've seen *too* many Males Pussy Sprung: chasing Pussy with the Knowledge that Females control Access to the Pussy; try chasing the **WOAMN...** that emotional Creature that, according to Street Law, ain't worth the Trouble or Drama.

As a Dom... and a hopeless Romantic... after you're Square internally, next comes Dealing with the **WOMAN.** This means to step back from the

Equation and observe, difficult for most **MALES**, no to mention someone with Control Issues.

As the **HOOD BORN** Dom, I use Street Lessons as a Guide; unfortunately, the Master finds a great deal of use for Pimpology. **NEVER Love no Hoe** is Standard Law... and one of the *many* Loop Holes is rather cruel: your Ol' Lady *is* your Bottom Bitch.

Where does Romance come when the Mentality is this? Nowhere... unless the Man is a Romantic by **NATURE**; otherwise it's more Game run on a Ho, chummers. This is where I Differ from Street-Taught and hardened Pimp... and where I am infinitely more dangerous than any Pimp. Most Pimps will quickly tell you how fickle and untrustworthy a Female is; I believe Differently: treat them as Human (in Praise *and* Punishment) if you would find Trust within a Female.

* * * *

Think about this odd sliver of Sprawl Fact: Cameras generally Focus on two Places: **Crossroads and Entrances**; now... Follow the Chaos Flow:

We Watch such Places because of one rude Human Expression: that's where Shit Happens. Entrances keep *some* out, and therefore, on the other side of *every* Entrance is something worth Concealing from **everyone**; Entrances protect The Unknown. As for the Crossroads, I choose this

Minority Goth - The Journey and Philosophy of One Black Man

Excuse: Humanity **NEEDS** to play Voyeur into the Thought-Processes of one another; this need filters over into a nagging itch to be One-Step-Ahead. Ahead of what?

The Unknown.

Many consider the Lifestyle a Journey into the Unknown; this is True **only at the Entrance to the Rabbit Hole**, the First Moment everything seemed *revealed*; often there is a very real sense of being blinded. However, there are a few Souls for which this Moment, the Moment of Discovery... Feels like **Confirmation**; these are curious Souls... and from them are Cast Gatekeepers; I am such a Gatekeeper.

They say we are Dark Souls, though they breathe/whisper of the Why Behind *only* when they are certain not even God is paying attention; we smile/Smile, though there is **always** Reason behind the Action. If we are Dark, it is because we have *much* to Think on, pondering things that are beyond Thought-Concept. Why? Because for some Reason (a matter of Faith, that) we can, it Feels Natural, and, personally...

There really isn't anything else to DO with Life except Live and Love; keep breathing and never give up Hope, you have a Chance of doing Both. However, because we as a Species are Human...

we've Evolved/Regressed to this point: ***WE CRAVE MORE!!!!!!!!!!***

    Gatekeepers Know and Understand this Truth: Crossing an Entrance Costs and **EVERYONE** Pays; the jaded ones Smile at those who wail and lament the Hidden Costs.

    Summed up in Sprawl-Speak: What are ya willin' to Pay to **survive** a trip Down the Rabbit Hole? Every Gatekeeper never worries about the Answer; they have their Payment ready; otherwise you would not be chattin' wi' 'em. **{{***That sound you here... is Indecision rummaging through your Thoughts and memories for Bargaining Items/Lies***}}**

* * * *

    I ain't Normal, and I'm very comfortable with this Fact and Truth; it frustrates *NORMAL* People to no damn end.

    And here, I find something Interesting: **if you believe you are Normal, I will offend/agitate/piss you off simply because I take another breath**; and I actually **Understand** this Logic-Flow; does not make it any less Wrong.

* * * *

    By Necropolis Standards it is Normal for Rich White Folk to be involved in the Lifestyle; a struggling Professional Cook with a Goal to be an Executive Chef, Mad Skillz, Talent and Ability, and

Minority Goth - The Journey and Philosophy

of One Black Man

this nagging Sense of Wanting/Needing to Find a Niche in his chosen Profession? Not even, and if the *nigga* starts Thinkin' in **any** Direction other than bein' some Female's Bitch-boy/Paycheck he really needs to be put in a round room. Of course... by those **same** Standards, any Female who wants to bed said nigga is a certified Psycho-Bitch. If she even **looks** like she believes (won't say Think here... because... well... Females Thinking... **ALL BAD!!**) that there is something else there... the Blind Excuse (think First Assumption here) is that she has a thing for Black Dick. If you see a shitload of Stereotypical nonsense, **WELCOME TO NECORPOLIS.**

Cuddling up to your Ol' Lady is Normal... except My Second... my Ol' Lady... Understands this: at **ANY** given Moment/Instant I will Take her; her Pleasure/Pain **while within Our Home** is at **MY** Will first, but *not* **only**; seize her by the hair and Fuck her silly... or nuzzle at her hair until I relax enough to fall asleep; for me, both require the same: **Blind Trust in a Female by my NATURALLY Paranoid Ass on Instinct.** And before you laugh/chortle/guffaw... ***I've had this once before.*** Mind... it **took** the arms, strength and Love of an Angel to **GET** it, but it was **VERY** REAL... and Worth Risking everything for; it was True Love; you never forget that Venom once it gets in the System... partially because it's infinitely more addictive than pure coke on its best day.

K.L. Miller

It ain't Normal for a Black Guy to **WANT or NEED** a Woman who doesn't find cockin'-up like a Bitch and pissing in the back yard during a sudden Summer rain storm at **ALL** disturbing (never mind THIS: *probably gonna be snarked that I don't have a golf umbrella as I fumble with my cell*)

It ain't Normal for a Black Male to have Ophidian, DJ Mad Dog, Nosferatu, Endymion, Angerfist, Tha Playah... **ANY** Hardcore/Hardstyle/Terrorcore DJ or DJ/MC Combo blaring in his personal headset, and most certainly *not* out where anyone else might chance to catch one of those Hi-Freq/distorted bass/missing-yet-Felt-as-an-itch Sounds. I am not supposed to Like those Sounds; I am supposed to stick to **some** of the Media Crap force-fed me: the crap that is edited Approved-for-Mass-Consumption (which is to say, you ain't gotta Think in order to Digest a damn thing). So when I'm In a Mood to hear hard Electronica, sip a chilled rocks glass half-filled with *good* rum, ponder over a few Tales as My Second gives me what is called in Da Hood **Slow Head while I Drive** (the Drive replaced by turning over just where this particular Tale is going, and if I Approve of the Direction, damn whether or not I Like it; occasionally I'll get bored and maybe **then** I'll pay her more Attention... or not)

* * * *

"There's somethin' *wrong* wit' dat boy..."

Minority Goth - The Journey and Philosophy

of One Black Man

Heard **that** a time or three infinities; the **CORRECT** Statement replaces ((wrong wit')) with *strange*. I like strange; homogeneous... tends to catch my Attention because it defies what I consider the Natural Order: Chaos.

In Necropolis, all of my Pack... Da Crew... those I consider *beyond* Family/Friends... were all a bit strange by (get ready) Normal Standards; perhaps it would be best to say Local Traditions. After all, highly intelligent Black Males who did not or could not dress in what Normal Standards considers Positive African American Role Model for the Period, *are gay.* You can ask me all damn day where this bullshit comes from and honestly... I could not tell you; what I *can* Speak on is the **pressure** to Conform to this bullshit; I Know it well; Feel it even now. So I'm reminded of this T-Shirt Saying: ***Conform, Go Crazy or Become an Artist***; right after that... Meatloaf Lyrics enter my Thoughts: "Two out of three ain't bad..."

The Wrong in that statement comes from this: ***I refuse to Conform!!!*** That is Wrong by Necropolis Standards; also happens to shatter Racial Barriers, but they politely ignore this. The Wrong comes from the stupidity of expecting and demanding Honesty and-slash-or the Truth from a Soul; in Necropolis, Polite is Right; it also hides the Fact that in your Heart-of-Hearts (such as it is these Days and Night), Dirty is an **understatement**; the typical Routine for a

Local is to fuck over everyone with a smile on your face... like mama and daddy taught you.

* * * *

Fred was confused; it overwhelmed him that his mother's new boyfriend wasn't upset at all about the MILF porno mag:

"Oh... so you'd rather he be out in da Streets fuckin' wi dez Silly Hos 'round here, huh?"

*Fred's confusion came from this: he thought he was odd because he **didn't** like Hood Rats/Ghetto Hoes/Thug Bitches; but, at least according to how his mother's black boyfriend was soundin'... his Point of View **won't that strange at all...***

"So... where the fuck are the other niggas like me?"

I could almost swap Fred for me... except for a few things.

Growing up, I was introduced to Black Porn as a *twisted* version of how far the Black Man had come. How? There were air-brushed Black Porn **STARS!!! ON THE COVER NO LESS; and they headlined those powerful all-white mags...** even the semi-pro stuff that most of the school kids *swore up and down had the best stuff!!!* Hey... it's the start of the Bible Belt, and the place where hypocrisy comes with every breath and thought; come right out with it, and at the time it kinda went :**God, Money, Pussy.** Of course, I was a bit pissed that **every** Black Male held the Big Dick **NIGGA** Image, and in today's porn, that Image seems to be the Best Seller. Makes perfect sense, since in Porn, *Stereotypes* Sell better; doesn't make me like looking at some schmuck's Schlong either.

Then there are Sex Toys; you cannot give such Items even a momentary nod in those Porn Novels that *no one* **EVER** reads or buys to a Child of the Dawning of the Techno-Geek Era; I spent *plenty* of Fantasies Thinking up some seriously Twisted Positions to use just a simple hard plastic vibrator on a Female. I developed a loathing for rigid vibrators the instant I touched one, and my first Latex one tickled Memories of Chemistry, Biology and ignited Thoughts of a Female and what **she** would Feel at her fingertips. It made Sense that *she* would know how it would feel inside her vagina... but just **who the fuck** spent their time in a lab thinking up the best feel for a Female? Seriously?!?!?

The same kind of sick fuck who wishes he'd Thought about tying a Female down and simply bringing her off until she passes out.

But **NOT** the Sick Fuck who, after reading a BDSM Porn novel that included *serious* Branding **by a Black Couple during Share Cropper Days**, becomes Intrigued by the Fact that the Male/Dom seemed so damned morose... and the submissive female, terrified of an end she seemed to crave, seemed **concerned** for the Health and Well-Being of the **THING** that Tormented her.

See... Fred is looking at MILF, a Standard of Middle America; she *used* to be White Blonde Female... until we started realizing that **MILF** was the best and most precise Term: **MOM**-I'd-Like-(to)-Fuck; race became a Non-issue, replaced by the fact that she'd given Birth. MILF is granted Experience, and thus, by Stupid-Gratis, Wisdom; of course, 2010 saw MILF become Cougar, and thus Humanity admits it animalistic ancestry/Instinct, but for now... **Fred wants himself a MILF.** And despite being Young and Hood-Raised Black-in-America... ***this makes Fred a Normal Schmuck like Joe Average!!!***

And here's the Twist: his Mom doesn't want her son looking at Glam-MILF... because of Claire Huxtable, the first Black MILF crammed down the throats of American Youths of **ALL** Racial Divides. If she has her Way, Fred and Tameka will Hook up, he'll get her pregnant and take care of the babies, cheat on her for a few years until he settles down (hopefully and, according to the Plan) with Tameka; and he'd **better** take care of all dem kids he got by who-knows-what-ho-he-been-wit; you may now go puke.

Stereotypes such as this are all too commonplace in Da Hood...

Minority Goth - The Journey and Philosophy of One Black Man

Illegals and the Lie of 18:

Illegals, as I Define the Term, are Teenagers; I call them Illegal because it is unlawful to Craft Tales about the Reality that all too many Homes/Houses face: **Teenage Sex.** Movies and such are fine within certain Limits, but the Printed Word is a completely different Creature. I've been warned about Posting my Illegal Tales because my Characters actually make their own Decisions; they may ask advice, or get it one way or another... or maybe they just Wing it. This, in my Opinion, is perfectly Natural, **since Mommy and Daddy cannot make the Decision, only Influence the Mind making it. In my Tales I place the awesome Power in the Hands of Teenagers...** and this frightens many.

So leave out the graphic stuff; this makes no sense. It completely dashes the possibility of Tom and Jane actually *enjoying* their first secretive encounter, and forbids Entry into the Rabbit Hole... and **HERE** I need only point to the plethora of Goth Chics who are *Teenagers... and ask about the many piercings.*

The Descent starts *somewhen...*; there is always a Beginning. What truly frightens many Adults is the possibility of their Teenager not just engaging in Sex, but dabbling or swimming in the deep, dark Kinky end of the Pool. As a Dom, I **DEFINITELY** take Notice... because **if** I have

Children, they will be Raised by a Dominant Father and a Mother who is My submissive... period. Look into the Mirror Darkly, for this will appear similar to a Traditional American Home. Mom makes the Rules which Dad the Bread Winner Enforces with (and **HERE** is where you get the differences, but that is a Subject for another Tale).

See... a Teenage Female, if you follow the Lie of 18, isn't supposed to have much more than Survival-Level Knowledge about Sex; Males are supposed to be sorting out their Feelings with Parental Guidance and other caring Adults.

* * * *

HERE is a terrifying REALITY:

Single mother in her Twenties, still eager to Hit the Clubs, or neck deep in School-for-a-Good-Career; toss in just *ONE* Other Guy/Step-Dad/Line-of-Whoevers...

Right there... Red Flags get snatched from hips; Females must be Heterosexual according to the Lie of 18; Lesbianism is Politely Ignored (I'll only State that once, since it is the Standard Excuse for anything not covered by the Lie)

Now... according to the Lie of 18, the Male is fully ready for Sex at 18. So is the Female; this is *supposed* to mean Mentally and Emotionally...

Minority Goth - The Journey and Philosophy
of One Black Man

You can stop the chuckling/laughter at any time, especially if Memories of an Illegal Romp flutter to mind; **every single Person who Lost their Cherry below the age of Eighteen is a Lawbreaker!!!** And if you did so and are Here/Now one of those Fuckheads force-believing the Lie of 18 because you had a bad experience... I say this:

Sadly... you are One of Many; that said... Pity is **not** what you need, so I will not pass its funk beneath your nostrils. Instead I offer this Scent for Thought: **choose One Soul dear to you... and influence them so that such a Thing is lessened in their Experience.**

Though, to take my own Words to Heart means Guiding an Illegal either Towards or Away from the Lifestyle and the Rabbit Hole.

And suddenly... I remember sneaking downstairs to watch Richard Pryor... Eddie Murphy... George Carlin... as a rising Illegal, that dangerous 10-to-12-year Age; my mother was busy Working the weekend shift again.

Actually, this is how I came to learn to Think of Fast Food as Hood Survival; her Employee Meal became the One Meal I ate all too often, School Lunch aside.

So... while I scarfed down left-over Fast Food... I Watched and Listened and Learned from raucous, raunchy, then-Real Humor; had to guess at quite a bit until I Learned that the other kids at School would whisper about what they'd seen, adding this and that. That was then...

Now? Tom whips out his Smart-Phone (the Family has a killer Plan, ya know?) and has Access to so much fraggin' info, even **with** the Parental Locks he probably knows thrice what we did at the same Rising Illegal Age (including where **NOT** to go and **WHY...** not to mention how to bypass those locks).

* * * *

And after all of the Knowledge is packed into Gray matter, one frightening Truth becomes all too clear: Knowledge is *Nothing* without Experience.

So long as this is True, that means People... **SOULS...** will be involved.

Guess it means that even as an Illegal I was right to see and Think about Guardians of Knowledge... and correct to See terrible Things within their Eyes, for they **knew** what lay in wait for me. Most Adults today are too busy scratching out an existence... busy Believing a Lie... whatever; those Souls seeking Experience are left to their own devices and harsh Realities. There is a lack of those Willing to Stand and Guard terrible Knowledge... or Guide those who, for whatever Reason/Excuse, simply must Know the Truth of Knowledge. Dare take this Position and many will consider you overly arrogant, taking a Role that this theirs...

* * * *

I Need a Slut as My Second; I figured this out during one Relationship where the Sex was killed because my Sex Drive was not only greater than my Ol' Lady, but I was just beginning another leg to my Journey Down the Rabbit Hole. She stopped me when I was close to bringing her to orgasm from Spanking; it pissed me off as well as surprised me. Spanking-as-Sex Play was, and still is, just another Tool in my shed.

But there's a misconception that must be clarified: as I Define a Slut, My Second must expend her Sexual Energies with ONE MALE; females are allowed into the Relationship only as Digi-Snacks: a shared experience. My Slut is not Out on the Streets; she doesn't need to seek Sexual Thrills outside of the Home. All she need do... is Ask the Twisted Mind within My Frame.

Burdens

Many consider this a Moment of Weakness and Vulnerability: tears flow freely down her cheeks as sobs sound out sorrow and anguish. Her head rests on my shoulder; her arms squeeze me tight, assured by the Human Form... and Comforted by the Soul and Essence within that Frame. I caress her back to ease the pain and tension within her, **NOT** because I'm setting myself up for Sorrow Pussy.

And... she's somewhat pissed that I **don't** at least make a *token* effort; I should be confused... but Time and Experience have taught me one thing: *she is here because I* **WILL NOT** *MAKE A Play for her...* Somehow, during such a Moment... Sex comes up. I'd almost say it's attached to the depth of Trust between us; Sounds Solid... and is something I must Ponder greatly...

Especially considering this Moment: she is illegal and comes to me for Advice, my Opinion, and-slash-or... Solace and a Title I've had since Childhood: Keeper of Secrets.

So... where does Sex come into this? The Father-Figure chummers; woe be to the Male in this Situation who is Blind to this; I... have a different Concern here, for I am a Dom.

You cannot keep such Information Hidden without dire consequences; Speaking Honestly will get one curious stares, the strangest *always* come from members of the Opposite Sex with either interest or, on some occasions, **experience** within the Lifestyle. I Craft Tales, so putting together a Scene for this is not just frightening, but stomps firmly upon Nerves. For simple example... her First Sex was Rough Sex and she frightened him because she wanted **MORE...**; age be damned, that Scene happens to be a Normal Entrance to the Rabbit Hole, one that spans Cultures, Traditions, Religion... every conceivable Human Category/Delineator.

And a Normal T-Monkey will probably just chalk it up to her being a Young Freak; as a Dom... I See much more. As a Man of Honor... there is concern for her Safety, and a nervous attention paid to making sure I do not Cross the Line.

There is also the Darkness and Shadows... and **they** Remember my Teenage Years; those were the Years of Stealth... when I spent much time exploring that ADS called Teenage Sex; if she doesn't try and Sneak a Over-Hug (one with a faked accidental Seductive Touch) or at least slither up and try to get to know me *outside*... I'd *really* be Concerned.

* * * *

It's been a shitty however-long-it's-been; right now... I'm looking forward to my bed, a *fat* bowl-pack and several glasses of rum. So of course the Shift ends with Server Drama and I get called as Security... which requires a level head first of all; I bring that, and a reputation of being one of Satan's Next-in-line Demons. Things quiet quickly... but I'm left chewing on more Fear from Servers.

"Come here; you need a Hug."

I Accept, but not before I let her see that Dark Thing growling softly behind my fixed Features.

So... the Hug has a certain Feel; if I had to describe it...

* * * *

She encircles my waist, laying her head gently on my Shoulder; the Moment is tender, rich with Human Compassion and honest, refreshing Caring...

I make Note of the Moment, Scanning for Who is keeping track of our movements; I recheck weapons-of-opportunity, adjusting my Style each nano-tick. Something other than Kitchen Drek has my Sense on edge. I feel her adjust her head... listening for my heartbeat. I smile...

Because I wonder if my Body has dampened the sound out of Street-Instinct... or if I've managed to keep it from teleporting back into my chest as I make certain to leave the Human Heart carefully tucked away in the darkest pit Nothing offers before each Shift; that means she's hearing a half-heart beating.

* * * *

"What's wrong?"

I smile and shake my head.

Minority Goth - The Journey and Philosophy

of One Black Man

"You need to get laid," she says quietly, Sadness touching the end-corner of her fading Words.

"True." And she is Taken... and a Good Woman.

Were I her Ol' Man... she wouldn't think twice about Sex for Stress Relief... so maybe that explains the wave of apparent jealousy... right before suggesting a co-worker she knows I've been at least Friendly with.

"So... you just go home and..."

"De-Rez. I'll work on a few Tales... putter online..." I end with a shrug, and a bemused grin tugging at my lips as I watched the sadness deepen within her.

"Hey... got no Ol' Lady to spend the time on... so..."

"Why not go out..." I raised my hand and chuckled softly, the Memory even now a darkly humorous Reminder...

"When I go Looking for something, I Find it... and a shitload more that I did not expect. So... I prefer the Happy Accident; it's been the safer Path... with a drekload less Drama, stress, and the other unnecessary bullshit most think is Standard issue in a Relationship these days."

* * * *

K.L. Miller

If the Master has an Alter-Ego...

Meanstreak - My Sight, My Soul

There is Tickle.

Then... there is...

* * * *

Do not Ask me Why; do not ask me anything.

Her tits are **MINE...** they are all that matter now. Here... I shall visit Pain upon her Flesh... Knowing it will spread until it touches her Soul...

And as I torment her... I'll ponder the Paths Pain takes; I'll study her for Trouble Signs...

But that is Within... **deep within... where she doesn't like to See...**

Her Thoughts are on the Surface Tension... the Aggression and Lust Powered grip.

"Human? Barely. Right now... all you Know is Pain. Fitting... and it is all you shall get from me... since it is what you are Here for. Correct?"

No answer is required; I Know. She Knows. I don't Lie... there is No Need.

So I let her cry... let her Experience her shame...

I'm trying not to let the Joker's sadistic grin deteriorate into sheer madness...

See... Under... I Experience something of a Joke: Go One Way... Man-Beast... the *other...* that Unholy thing known as Man. And Man **enjoys** the whimpering Woman sinking to her knees, hissing as I tighten the short length of dog chain around one tit, distending it...

"Nice... Tone?"

One. Twice. Three...

Careful... Emotion in that Blow... got a Dick-Pulse.

Fitting; she looked at it, eyes glazed over; **nothing Human within this Frame... a Shell... a Living Fuck Toy...**

Bit disobedient... so... Training...

* * * *

Honest Freak here; if you're looking for Sucka... next Nigga in Line; want a Paycheck... I'm just a hard workin' Cook trying his best to let the **FOOD** do the Talkin' and Memory Makin'. I don't want or **NEED** to be so damn filthy fuckin' Rich that everyone envies me... that people despise me for the Dazzle they covet.

Honest Freak here; you don't want or need a Cuddle Whore... fine by me; sometimes I really don't want my Dick anywhere **near** you... all I Require is a Warm, Loving **SOUL** Within Human Flesh. Sometimes a Cuddle is sexier than lingerie and a Big-ol'-Butt... the *capacity* to let someone ***<u>get that damn close for that damn long!!!!!!!!!!</u>***

Lost in The Streets... Da Hood; Temporary *everything...*

No Time to spend on Simple Pleasure... so...

* * * *

Some Males Require **someone** to Maintain certain aspects of their Existences; **MEN** call them Bitch-Ass, Punks, other derogatory terms... and I agree... somewhat.

If you **NEED** someone... get them; find someone to fill the Position... yet **always** with an Eye to **YOUR HAPPY ASS BEING TOP DOG!!!!!!!!**

PUSSY-AZZ NIGGAZ... and this Term is Racially unbiased... have one ***<u>specific</u>*** Why behind their Actions: Pussy. It's **all** about Pussy... Sex dominates their Existence and the Females know it: Feed the Beast and they've got a Pet...

Minority Goth - The Journey and Philosophy of One Black Man

Strange thing about these Females... **they prefer Dogs... then BITCH about their performance...**

Sounds like Trainer Issues to me; then again... Bitches Teaching Bitches... what's to be expected.

* * * *

There's a Look I get when someone Fucks with m'Money...

Here is what it Feels like:

Within this Shell there are Two Essences: Mine... and God.

Were it not for God Reminding me of the Human Soul... His Precious Creation... the Form before me would have nano-seconds to Live before Termination of Life Functions. I Required Information and m'Money... everything else... Collateral Damage...

* * * *

I'm not supposed to Listen to their Hopes and Dreams; I'm not supposed to Play Along when they seem desperate to Live a Fantasy.

I'm supposed to be the Strong Black Man... rigid-stiff ex-Playa GQ Schmoove...

I'm not supposed to find Beauty in a Woman bound by rope... chains... leather; I'm not supposed to find Comfort and Pleasure in stroking **My Pet's** Hair (not My Wife or Ol' Lady...)

Throw a Big Booty in my face... Bit Tits on a Black Queen (gold diggin' heifer who checked out my Gear to see if I could afford her...)

Hey... I **do** have a passable Mean Mug; I'm often seen in something *similar* to Street Gear (if I'd **only** get rid of the Gothic slant to things and Wear gang Colors, Hip-Hop Gear and the other Trappings...)

Listen up; I ain't Repeatin' this shit: **I Keep it 100**.

When I say Color doesn't matter... it doesn't; only the SOUL means shit to me and if it's foul and fetid it Serves no Purpose... and I'll dismiss your sorry ass... Color be damned. This is Who and What I am and I'll be THRICE DAMNED if I stick dick in **any** Female based only on the Color of her Skin; don't like it... not your *fuckin'* Problem, breeder; Buzz...; I've got Shit to Do and I'm a bit behind.

Is there a Black **WOMAN** capable of fitting my Standards? **SURE!!!!!!!** But I do not expect this Rare Gem to find me without serious Effort on BOTH parts. Besides... according to the **NORM** I'm so Rare that I should not Exist. No Charges... no Kids... Working... and **SINGLE?!?!?!** Got the same Struggles... same Bills... same Grind, chummers; that won't Change so long as Human Society Exists.

Minority Goth - The Journey and Philosophy of One Black Man

If there **is** something *wrong* with me... it is this: I don't Push Up on Cuties; I prefer to Talk with Intelligent Women. I don't Break Backs-Don't Call; I'd rather Spend Time with My Ol' Lady/Second. **HOME** gets taken care of **FIRST**; I ain't worried about what goes on in the Streets.

* * * *

I **LOVE** Hardcore.

Nearly everyone around me looks at me as if I'm a Freak for enjoying the high-Freqs and distorted bass... Trip-Sets and Aggressive, Angry...

Surprisingly Minority Goth Lyrics... most ripped from RAP!!!!!!

Now... I Know this won't get me Points with Black Females... but I really don't dig the Booty Music... and **not** because of the self-degradation implied within the Lyrics...

It's the Ho Mentality in general: Hear bass... ass-out and GO!!!

Instinct.

This... *bothers* me.

Sheep, yo... **SHEEP!!!**

* * * *

"Why not rant on Black **MALES?!?!?!?!?**"

Easy: most are Dead, In Jail... or wallowing in Solitude... *single...* because someone fragged him over One-Time-Too-Many.

Few **MEN** left; and from this speck... you choose to select only a certain colored Facet...

Few **MEN** left means the Next Generation has Fewer Teachers... Good **or** Bad...

And... we've gotta Bling in order to Attract Female... then select Good Woman from that...

Yeah... the complete Shit-pile we've created for ourselves as a Species.

So Pardon this Black Man if he's a bit harsh on his Judgment; trying **not to** is so difficult when you are scrutinized constantly... **and constantly found Lacking by those who claim Interest... Feign Love.**

* * * *

ADS:

You're supposed to be able to Throat Fuck a Slut and you're **supposed** to enjoy it...; you are not supposed to get this from your Wife... the Woman You Love; she is never a Slut.

Anyone ever ask **HER?**

Seriously?

Already Know the Answer... if ya go by Normal Standards: *fuck NO!*

Bullshit... but that's the crap I gotta deal with; I firmly believe MILF, every now and again, wants and Needs Sex-sans-Love from the Man she Loves...

No idea about the Why behind... just Commenting on one fucked up *Excuse* for Females Cheating: not gettin' so-called Good Lovin' (Freaky Sex) at Home...

Because I **can't** convince Guys that their Ol' Ladies like this shit; easier to be Back Door Man, bus' yo Ol' Lady Cock-eyed and silly, jack yo Crib and bail on da Silly Ho. Roll a Blunt 'n Forget About It...

* * * *

I think about this. Often.

If you know squat about me... and suddenly... I have an Ol' Lady...

You Know she's a Certified Pain Slut... *A FREAK!!!!!!*

Takes a **Strong Woman** to deal with this; probably Why I don't do Girls, Hoochies, Dingbats, Church Goin' Females of **any** Color/Affiliation...

Which bring me to **this**: the Black Freak *Stereotype...*

Still a **FEMALE...; still Human...**; I say this:

She doesn't Grow Out of *Being a Freak*; she **Seasons...**; odds favor her Significant Other is not only Wise but sexually adventurous... **bare minimum!!!** I See and Know nothing Wrong with this... quite the contrary if Love is the Foundation of the Relationship.

With this said... ***KEEP THE CHURCH OUT OF THE SEX LIFE FOR THE LOVE OF ALL GET OUT!!***

Note My Word Choice... I did **NOT** say ***GOD.***

Within My bedroom... **GOD** has a very Real Presence...; the **CHURCH** can keep it's nosy, gossip-fueled Judgments to themselves and be content to finger-fraggin' themselves to Fantasies of this:

GOD Given Pleasure; it ain't Evil... **THOUGHT** ain't evil...

Sex is a Tool... a Tool ***for Mankind's Use.***

So. Use... **not** Abuse; requires Wisdom. That Requires Knowledge... ***Experience...*** and careful Thought and Consideration... of even the Impossible; ain't easy...

Hence, in my Opinion, Why Things like the Church gripes at Sex in general: Hard Work for

Enlightenment that goes Beyond the Physical... smacks of Touching a sliver of God in a different Way... Different Path; uncomfortable Notion for many so-called Traditional Southern Church-Raised Black Females...

Many Me's

Here's a Thought:

The Do Gooder met a submissive Woman... Fell In Love... and the Dom Within Expressed.

<u>Under NO circumstances is this, or My Existence, the NORM!!!</u>

Given the presence of this thing we call Normalcy I am but One Possible Outcome.

* * * *

This guy figured out he could use Kinky Sex and a passable Dom Mask to snag Miss Home Body; now his Ol' Lady, a submissive Woman, is quite literally Stuck. Not because of any perceived or actual violence or True Dom/sub Relationship...

See... submissives ALSO Follow a Code; and a submissive does **NOT** betray their Master... even if said Betrayal is the only Way to ensure their continued Safety.

* * * *

This makes the Second Case Pure Street Sad; the Guy Expressed alright, but he wants a fraggin' *harem!!!*

Unfortunately... that won't fly in his Social Circles *unless* he Marries... which she **does** want; the Other Women? ***NEVER AGAIN...***

Can someone say CNN News Special about Domestic Violence?

And Why Street Sad? Chummer... I've seen **this** Scene play out in Da Club... ***with every fraggin' Playa I've ever laid eyes on!!!***

* * * *

This one...

From the one he Fell in Love with comes this Horrid venom-Thought: *all* Females are nothing more than Sluts and Whores... ***CUNTS!!!***

So if this fuck-head *finds* a Female willing to co-exist with him... chances are she is Weak... ***NOT SUBMISSIVE!!!!!!!!!!!!***

Minority Goth - The Journey and Philosophy of One Black Man

This is nothing more than Hate's Downward Spiral; she cannot stop it... **he must make the Effort... and he refuses**; she is there to Experience all of the sordid whatevers... Why? Ask her... is she makes it out.

So pardon the Dom in me when some twit remarks about the chains and other Bondage items... *claiming ALL FREAKS are gonna end up like that*; just an Impulse to show them stark Proof of their Stupidity.

* * * *

From Twisting the Lifestyle into a *Game Plan...* to the most bizarre C.S.I. Standard Issue Domestic Violence Mystery, **_anything is Possible..._**

Not every **Man** is a Dom; if a Man calls himself a Dom, **_first_** he must **be** a **_REAL MAN..._** and you can discard all burly, muscular Images; this deals with the **SOUL** within the Frame, not the Dazzle/Maybe-Lie.

MEN have no Need to Lie to their Ol' Ladies; Doms work hard to strip away Lies from their submissives... Single and Chosen or the Stable Kept. And whether One or Many... a True Dom *INSTINCTIVELY* Pays Attention to **every** Detail.

So the Stable Lord *knows* when one is getting Too Close... and Knows if **he** is getting too close...

she is...; he Knows these Distances with a Touch that defies the Physical. He'd better... or he'll soon find his Stable in disarray... if not a complete ruined heap.

One-on-One Doms... kinda have it easier; there's a **shitload** of Data about that and it all comes down to Street Lore: ***TAKE CARE OF HOME FIRST!!!***

These... EVEN BROKE, struggling financially, Hustlers and Minority Goth... these tend to **NEED...** and Strive for this Title:

Lord of the Manor.

Daddy Ain't Home

Spring Fever: *Side Effects include the Ol' Man NOT having enough energy to Fuck Mommy like the Spring Love/Sex/Breed Biological Cycle Dictates...*

I blame this on Society... the Crap Mankind started the instant this thing called Intelligence became the In-Thing. I hear it now more than ever... especially from MILFs with Significant Others Punching Clock wherever/wherever; funny thing is...

Minority Goth - The Journey and Philosophy

of One Black Man

* * * *

Here is the **MALE Created Here/Now Tradition:** Work... de-stress *away* from the Home (remember that **WORD:** *__HOME__*)

Now... once Home... Things Run Smoothly; Life happens...

Anyone else see the **complete** Gloss-over? Every sexually frustrated MILF... *__Female...__ Knows this Gloss-Over Area painfully TOO well;* at **some** Point she Gets Dick **but then Pumps Out a Unit.**

No Passion, chummers.

No Attention to Detail.

Mommy is a Machine; she Serves a Purpose.

She ain't Human... so don't Apply such terms as Woman or Lady; as a Machine, Negative Terms will do (in 'Polite'/Familiar Company).

Won't be long before **Home** is **House...** *__a Thing.__*

This is never Good for Family; Family Requires a *__HOME__*; this means Daddy's gotta Pay Attention to Detail... **BE** a bit paranoid... *functionally* Paranoid... about the seemingly unimportant... **THE LITTLE THINGS.**

Like Boredom... the slight itch that T-Monkey Theory says all she needs is Sex...

Not *quite* True... because of this: **treat every Female as an Individual...**

Don't Know your Ol' Lady... you're Guessing and chances favor you Guess Wrong, chummers.

* * * *

And T-Monkeys are steady on this Paper-Chase...

Materialism taking the Place of everything else... and the grinding Acceptance Society struggles with; somewhere... Males are **supposed** to Fall-in-Line and...

What ever happened to **Take Care of Home** within the entire mish-nosh of the Paper Chase? Got lost in Short-Term Pleasure and I can't say it's because Today's Mind cannot contemplate Tomorrow...; ***THEY ARE TERRIFIED THAT TOMORROW BRINGS A CESSATION TO THEIR ENJOYMENT OF PLEASURE!!!!!!!!!!!!*** Toss in the *slightest* Punishment for this Enjoyment... and it goes from dismal to this: Now I understand the hedonistic urges... **Fear of the Unknown... Fear of Tomorrow.**

Hollow Existence.

Share. Grow. Learn. **TOGETHER!!!!!!!!! It can be done if you're willing to give up the glitz and**

glam and forget the Judgment of your Peers as you Seek Happiness Within your Own universe... and those surrounding you.

For all too many... it's the Flash-and-Glitz Media-fed *this is what you SHOULD be Wanting*; and I do not see Ol' Lady in that Picture... just a plethora of Pussy on parade.

And so... Mommy is left to Deal with her Itch; that's **ALL** the Warning I'm givin' the T-Monkey's Chasin' Paper... especially those Ego twits who **think** because they're breathing every Female is **THEIR** Pussy...

Chummer... just Speakin' Street... *keep Sleepin'... **stupid.***

Smoke and Shadows

Editing Minority Goth... trying not to Dream of the Bright Lights; I've heard the Horror Stories... Know something of the Dangers...

But each Night I go to bed I Pray to God for many things... and one of them is a way out of Necropolis... *again.* Education helped before... maybe it will do so again...

Dance with the One that Brung ya; Local Colloquialism and Brutal Truth.

When Writing a Book was nothing more than Idle Fantasy, I was afraid of what others would Think; now...

It's not that I don't care...

I've grown to understand the place of Peer Judgment and Criticism.

* * * *

I don't think I'll ever go for Flashy; too used to the Shadows.

So when I'm Famous... you'll probably ignore me as I ghost past... the only Sign of Wealth...

My Duster and Levi's carpenter jeans; Name Brands equals Money in Da Hood...

And Da Hood **is** Where I Feel Comfortable...

And yes... that Ideal Community where you get along with your neighbors, the Cops **are** allies and **not** unwanted intruders... **DA HOOD.**

What Shadows Exists in that Image?

Daddy wants his Dick Sucked... Momma wants someone to Tap-Dat-Ass...

Sex, chummers; until we decide Public orgies are like Grass Growing: natural and accepted as such... it **will** Happen within dark rooms... and there **will** be Dark Thoughts...

And Sunlight alone cannot Banish these...

* * * *

I am 39; Minority Goth is ageless... and in Da Hood, Minority Goth is now Illegal... a Teenager... Pre-Teen...

I never carried a pistol; Illegals think themselves **naked** without Heavy-Duty Bang-Bang tucked on them... *and they're just changing Class in School!!!*

I used to Craft Tales within the Shadowrun™ Universe to pass the Time... and maintain Sanity during my Life in the Big Easy... and Imagined such a Day; the Imagination is a truly Powerful Weapon and often dwarfed in Horror by Cold Reality...

In Da Hood... in **Society...** the Greatest Super Villain is capable of Controlling your Thoughts, and isn't Limited by Technology...

Today... **FEAR** is the Villain...

And the **only** Way to Defeat Fear is with Knowledge and Wisdom ***together...***

But... the only Way to get it is to go through some Serious Shit; it will Scar the Soul... and **that** will Show...

BUT... get it and you won't Need Guns; Get it... and you won't have Fear in your Heart.

And you'll Face those Wielding Fear... Screaming at you... begging you to Join Them... Be sheep... Follow the Masses... **and above all DO NOT THINK FOR YOURSELF!!!!**

That leads to a Suffering that Normals do not understand... only Fear-by-Instinct.

* * * *

In the End... this is One Black Man's odd Tale of Living by a Code of Honor within Da Hood... a Sliver of Society that has a different View... and in that...

This Book is Nothing New to anyone.

Funny that...

Shadows Guard you all.

Minority Goth - The Journey and Philosophy of One Black Man

Fin

ABOUT THE AUTHOR

Born the Child of a Single Mother, K.L. Miller is a talented Writer, gifted Professional Cook and self-professed Street Philosopher. He is a Hero to some and a Protector to others, his heart of gold, neatly hidden behind his tough exterior Spending most of his formative years in South Central Virginia (*Necropolis*) and the New River Valley (*The CDZ*), he would gain Street Experience within two Cities during the height of their Popularity/Infamy: Los Angeles - City of Lost Angels and New Orleans – The Big Easy, his adopted Home (*only call it Big **SLEAZY** if you're Local, ya 'eard!*) A Survivor of Hurricane Katrina, the Tragedy figures prominently in his Tales.